THE SLIMMER'S
MICROWAVE COOKBOOK

THE SLIMMER'S
MICROWAVE COOKBOOK

Margaret Weale

DAVID & CHARLES
Newton Abbot London North Pomfret (Vt)

Photography by Stan Weale
The author is grateful to Rackhams, Birmingham, for kindly lending many
accessories used in the food photography

British Library Cataloguing in Publication Data

Weale, Margaret
    The slimmer's microwave cookbook.
    1. Reducing diets—Recipes
    I. Title
    641.5′635   RM222.2

    ISBN 0-7153-8392-2

Phototypeset by ABM Typographics Limited, Hull
and printed in the Netherlands
by Smeets Offset BV, Weert
for David & Charles (Publishers) Limited
Brunel House   Newton Abbot   Devon

Published in the United States of America
by David & Charles Inc
North Pomfret   Vermont 05053   USA

Contents

Introduction

As a child I was brought up in true Scottish tradition, and the hearty meals, eaten regularly each day were reflected in my sturdy, well-built appearance. In particular, the variety of calorie-laden, home-baked bread, scones, cakes, shortbread and pastries served for afternoon and high tea, in addition to the steamed suet puddings served for lunch, were unknowingly neither good for my health nor my figure. Having a mother and grandmother who were both expert cooks and bakers meant that food dominated our lives, and we tended to live to eat, rather than to eat to live. This was supposedly a good way of living and a sign of affluence, and the fact that it might be unhealthy was never considered.

Growing up in this type of environment I, too, became interested in food and decided to follow a career in the field of Home Economics. This meant leaving home, and it was during my years of study that my attitude to food, and life, changed. I became interested in nutrition and the effect of food on our health and bodies, and decided it was time to change my own way of eating and to lose weight. This I did, and many years later I still follow this healthier eating pattern and have no desire to return to my former eating habits.

As a practising professional Home Economist, as well as a wife and mother, food still dominates my life, but in a different way. I thoroughly enjoy cooking and eating, but I am neither interested in, nor tempted by, calorie-laden recipes. Having experienced the joy and pleasure of being slim, fit and healthy—and able to wear fashionable clothes with confidence—I follow an eating pattern which suits my lifestyle and yet enables me to maintain my body weight. Counting calories daily, and weighing on the same day each week with the rest of the family, are established and worthwhile habits.

Many basic foods are not, in themselves, high in calories. Their bad reputation as fattening foods is often the result of what we add to them, or perhaps even more important, the way we cook them. My professional and personal interest in food now centres around developing recipes and cooking techniques which avoid these unnecessary additions or methods, yet provide menus which offer maximum eating pleasure for minimum calories.

The microwave oven has made this possible in so many ways and has opened up a whole new world for me and the many people who want to be slim and stay slim. Remember, losing weight is one thing, maintaining weight is another. If you revert back to your former high-calorie, unhealthy way of cooking and eating, you will quickly regain lost weight. However, with the help of a microwave cooker and continued sensible eating, you can look forward to a lifetime of healthier, more enjoyable eating which will make you, your family and friends wonder how you can remain so slim while enjoying food which looks and tastes so good—and was cooked in minutes rather than hours.

The exciting world of slimming

According to current research, about half the people in this and other western-style societies weigh more than is good for them and feel the need to do something about it. Not surprisingly, therefore, among any small gathering of friends invariably at least one is either on a diet, or has been on a diet, or has decided to go on a diet. Slimming groups and clubs up and down

Ratatouille (page 83)

6

the country are well supported, diets and slimming are topics for discussion whatever the occasion, books galore have been written and magazines publish special articles on the subject, advertisements for slimming aids are everywhere and the medical profession emphasises that being overweight is unhealthy—so advice and information on diet is delivered from all sides.

OVEREATING

You are what you eat: this is a startling thought, especially when you realise that the average person swallows about half a ton of food, excluding drink, each year. In recent years there has been a greater general tendency to over-eat, and although our bodies are remarkably efficient, tolerant machines, they can only cope up to a point, beyond which the results of over-indulging eventually shows in the form of excess weight which can effect your health as well as your appearance.

OVERWEIGHT

If you are carrying excess weight, not only will you have difficulty in choosing fashionable clothes, but more seriously you may be more prone to, or suffer from, some of the illnesses associated with obesity—shortness of breath, varicose veins, backache, high blood pressure, and others too frightening to mention. For your health's sake as well as vanity, it is therefore essential to control your body weight.

No-one *cannot* lose weight. If, however, you have any doubts about your general health, it is advisable to consult a doctor before embarking on a slimming regime.

For most of us, eating is one of life's pleasures, but it is possible to adjust our eating pattern to get slimmer, rather than fatter, while forming good, healthy, enjoyable eating habits to last a lifetime.

CALORIES

Fats and fatty foods provide calories in their most concentrated form and are the most fattening foods of all. A very small quantity of fat supplies a very large number of calories, so by reducing the total amount of fat in our food we can considerably reduce our total calorie intake. From a health point of view most doctors agree that by reducing the amount of fat (particularly animal fat) we eat, we can help to prevent the build-up of cholesterol in the blood.

CARBOHYDRATES

Many sugary and starchy carbohydrate foods are high in calories, although weight for weight they are not as high as fats. Sugar is the most concentrated form of carbohydrate and provides no other nutrients—it is purely a source of energy, supplying 'empty' calories which can be detrimental to health and weight. Most foods which have a high sugar content, such as cakes, biscuits and chocolate, also tend to have a high fat content, so they too should be strictly limited in the slimmer's diet. Starchy foods, such as breakfast cereals (without sugar), flour, bread and root vegetables, including potatoes, supply nutrients as well as essential fibre and can therefore be included, within limits.

PROTEIN

Everyone needs protein for body construction and repair, but an adult needs less than a growing child, and on average we eat more than we really need. Many protein foods, such as some meat, hard and cream cheese, also contain a deceptively high amount of fat. For this reason it is advisable to choose lean cuts of meat and the lower calorie cheeses, such as edam, austrian smoked, brie, camembert, and cottage cheese. Eat more fish, especially white fish, and poultry, all of which contain less fat.

VITAMINS AND FIBRE
Fresh fruit and vegetables are wonderful foods for healthy eating, because as well as being low in calories, they also supply vitamins, essential fibre and roughage.

MINERALS
On average there is no shortage of minerals in a varied western-style diet, but for those who may need extra iron, low-calorie foods such as liver and kidneys, and leafy green vegetables like spinach are good sources.

Reducing waist and waste with a microwave oven

A microwave oven is a most valuable aid to slimming. It enables you to prepare healthy, low-calorie, enjoyable meals quickly, conveniently and economically, whether you are cooking for one, for the family, or for guests when entertaining.

Many foods, which normally require the addition of calorie-laden fat to prevent sticking during conventional cooking, can be cooked without fat in a microwave oven. Other foods have fat added for flavour during or after conventional cooking. Again, this is unnecessary in a microwave oven because foods cook in their own juices which improves their flavour and makes them more appetising and satisfying.

Since food cooked in a microwave oven is moist, juicy and full of flavour, there is no longer the need for calorie-laden thick gravies or rich sauces. Low-calorie, fat-free, lump-free sauces are, of course, quickly and easily made when the occasion arises.

The speed of cooking combined with the reduction in the amounts of liquid, especially when cooking vegetables, means maximum retention of vitamins and minerals, which in turn provides healthier, more nutritious food.

The way in which microwaves cook food and the speed at which they do so means that neither time nor energy are wasted. Nutritious low-calorie foods can be ready to eat in minutes, so there is no temptation to reach for a high-calorie fattening snack when hunger strikes or when eating alone. Individually packed portion-controlled foods are a boon to slimmers and can be speedily defrosted, reheated or cooked as required. Less time spent in the kitchen means more time for other pursuits, including exercise.

Left-over food or drink (coffee) need not be wasted. They can be quickly reheated in the oven and taken out looking and tasting as if freshly cooked or made.

The facility to cook a wide variety of appetising low-calorie foods quickly, economically, and without fuss, prevents diet boredom and offers one of the easiest ways to lose weight.

Recipes throughout this book make use of the calorie-reduced foods now available. These include skimmed milk, natural low-fat yoghurt, low-fat cottage cheese, low-fat spread, artificial sweeteners, natural fruit juice, fruit canned in natural juices, low-calorie sauces and dressings, as well as foods recommended for the slimmer.

A calorie count is given for each recipe. This can only be approximate since products from various manufacturers have a different number of calories for the same weight, but it will give general guidance.

Welcome to the exciting world of slimming and enjoy it.

The microwave oven

Although microwave ovens have been used in the catering industry for many years, it is only recently that domestic models have become increasingly popular, in this country at least. Sales of domestic microwave ovens are steadily increasing as more and more people become aware of their many advantages and realise that they are one of the most practical and invaluable assets in the home. With their time- and energy-saving features they are a sound investment. In this age of convenience and frozen foods, the microwave oven makes fast foods even faster. Used in conjunction with a conventional cooker and home freezer, it reduces the time spent in the kitchen to a minimum and although cooking will never be completely effortless, the microwave oven makes it faster, easier and more enjoyable.

A wide variety of models by several manufacturers is now available, and although individual designs and features may differ, the basic principles of microwave cookery remain the same.

POWER OUTPUT

The higher the power output of an oven the faster it cooks, and vice versa. Most ovens now have at least two power output controls which allow you to cook quickly at full power, and defrost or cook more slowly at a lower setting. Some ovens offer variable power or selector control which provides the user with a variety of output levels from which to choose.

POWER OUTPUT LEVELS

The recipes and timings given in this book were tested in ovens with maximum power outputs of 600–700W. Only two settings, or power output levels, are used throughout the book and they represent the power output levels most commonly found on the control panels of most ovens.

Setting	Approx percentage of microwave energy	Approx power output
HIGH	100%	600–700W
LOW	30–50%	200–300W

OVENS WITH LOWER POWER OUTPUT

Ovens with maximum power outputs of less than 600W need extra time. The charts below will enable you to adjust the times in this book, but be sure to read the manufacturer's instructions supplied with your oven and check the percentages and power outputs above.

600–700W ovens ★	500–600W ovens	400–500W ovens
¼ min	17 sec	20 sec
½ min	35 sec	41 sec
1 min	1 min 9 sec	1 min 21 sec
2 min	2 min 22 sec	2 min 42 sec
3 min	3 min 27 sec	4 min 3 sec
4 min	4 min 36 sec	5 min 24 sec
5 min	5 min 45 sec	6 min 45 sec
10 min	11 min 30 sec	13 min 30 sec
15 min	17 min 15 sec	20 min 15 sec
20 min	23 min 00 sec	27 min 00 sec
25 min	25 min 45 sec	33 min 45 sec
30 min	34 min 30 sec	40 min 30 sec

★ As used to test recipes and timings in this book

Stuffed Rainbow Peppers
(page 85)

TIMING

Times given for defrosting, reheating and cooking food must be used as a helpful guide only, since specific time required will vary between models. The actual time required, as already explained, will be affected by the power output of the oven. It will also be affected by the following factors:

1 The size, shape and type of cooking dish used and the arrangement of food in the oven.
2 The size, shape and starting temperature of the food, and the depth of food in the dish. Remember, food taken from the refrigerator will take longer to cook than food at room temperature.
3 The amount of food used. When quantities are increased, cooking time is increased accordingly; likewise, by decreasing the quantities, less time is required for cooking. As a guide, when the amount of food is doubled, the time should be increased by about one-half and the food then checked for readiness. Similarly, should you wish to halve a recipe, you should reduce the time by between one-half and one-third.
4 Quality of ingredients. As with conventional cooking, the acceptability of the end results will depend on the quality of the ingredients used.
5 Personal preference. Times given may be increased or decreased to suit individual taste.

Remember, it is always advisable to underestimate the time required for defrosting, reheating or cooking food by microwave energy. Food can always be returned to the oven for additional time, but there is no remedy for spoiled or overcooked food.

Experiment with one or two recipes in this book, test the food regularly, and make any necessary adjustment to the times given. Other recipe timings can then be adjusted accordingly. To begin with, use the exact quantities given in each recipe in order to establish the preferred timing for optimum results.

Containers and utensils

COOKING CONTAINERS

A microwave oven allows you to use a far wider variety of cooking containers than a conventional oven, and since food does not burn on, they are much easier to clean. You can often use the same dish for cooking and serving, so saving time heating serving dishes and washing up.

You will no doubt find that you already possessed a variety of suitable casseroles, dishes and bowls made of ovenproof glass or pottery in your kitchen before you purchased your microwave oven.

TESTING CONTAINERS

It is easy to determine whether or not a container is suitable for microwave use. Simply place the container in the oven with a glass of water and microwave on HIGH for 1 min. If the container is suitable, it will remain cool while the water will be warm. However, if the container is warm, it has absorbed microwave energy and should not be used. Do not place cups with glued handles in the oven—glue melts.

METAL

Generally, containers and utensils made of metal or having a metallic trim or metal signature on the base should not be used in the microwave oven. Metal reflects microwave energy and can cause arcing. There are, however, exceptions to every rule. Foods packed in foil containers less than 2cm (¾in) in depth can be used, provided they are full of food and do not touch the surfaces of the oven interior. Aluminium foil may be used in small quantities to shield the small thinner areas or parts of food to slow down their rate of defrosting, reheating or cooking, but must not touch the oven's interior surfaces.

Foil-lined containers, such as some milk cartons, should not be placed in the oven. Foil wrappings must be removed from butter, and metal twist ties should be removed from bags and replaced by loosely tied string or an elastic band.

Metal skewers can be used only if there is a large proportion of meat to skewers. Wooden skewers are preferable.

PAPER AND PLASTICS
Paper napkins, towels, cups and plates can be used for short cooking times. Kitchen paper is often used in the microwave oven to absorb moisture or fat.

Dishwasher-safe plastics are normally suitable for low-temperature cooking, but are not recommended for cooking foods with a high sugar or fat content. Tupperware is not advised.

Plastic wrap or clingfilm is widely used in microwave cookery to form a sealed cover to retain heat and moisture. Roasting and cooking bags should be split or pierced to allow steam to escape and prevent bursting, and be loosely tied with string or an elastic band.

STRAW AND WOOD
Straw and wicker baskets can be used for the very short times required to heat bread or rolls.

Wood has a tendency to dry out during prolonged periods, but wooden spoons can be left in containers for short periods, although they may get hot.

MICROWAVE BROWNING DISH OR GRILL
This utensil is specially designed to sear and brown foods such as chops, steaks and beefburgers in a microwave oven. Follow the manufacturer's instructions for pre-heating and cooking, and always handle with oven gloves.

MICROWAVE OVEN THERMOMETERS
These are specially designed for use in microwave ovens. Conventional meat thermometers must not be used in the oven, but can be used in food after it has been removed from the oven.

SPECIAL MICROWAVE CONTAINERS AND UTENSILS
An ever-increasing variety of containers and utensils is available, in a wide range of shapes, sizes and materials. Some can be used not only in the microwave oven but also in conventional ovens and/or freezers. Choice depends on individual requirements.

SHAPES AND SIZES OF COOKING CONTAINERS
The shape and size of cooking container and the depth of food in it will affect the speed of cooking and the attention necessary during defrosting, reheating or cooking, as well as the end result.

For the most even heating and cooking, round dishes are best. The next best results are produced in square dishes with rounded corners. The least successful are rectangular-shaped dishes. Shallow dishes are the most efficient, but it is often necessary to use deep dishes to prevent spillage in the oven. Straight-sided dishes are better than those with sloping or tapering sides.

Ring moulds give good results and are especially effective when food cannot be stirred. If you do not have a ring mould you can place a glass jar or tumbler in the centre of a suitable dish to produce the same effect.

Microwave cooking techniques

A microwave oven, like any other appliance, has its limitations, but it also has special features which make it different. As with any method of cooking, end results will depend on the care and attention given to the food before and during its time in the oven, whether it is being defrosted, reheated or cooked, and the quality of the basic ingredients.

SIZE AND SHAPE OF FOOD

When you cook a stew or casserole conventionally, you know that the larger pieces of meat and vegetables take longer to cook. The same applies to cooking by microwave energy, so for even cooking it is important to cut food into even-sized pieces. Larger pieces will also take longer to defrost or reheat than smaller pieces. Boned and rolled joints of meat cook more evenly than joints with bone, and poultry cooks more evenly when it is well trussed.

QUANTITY OF FOOD

Increasing the quantity of food increases the time taken to defrost, reheat or cook it.

COVERING FOOD

As with any form of cooking, food must be covered when steam and moisture are to be retained. In a microwave oven, food cooks more quickly and evenly with a tightly sealed cover, such as clingfilm, than with a loose lid. Dry baked foods are not normally covered.

STIRRING AND TURNING

Since microwaves start cooking food around the outside of the dish first, it is often necessary to stir during cooking to bring the cooked food from the out-side to the centre and the less cooked food from the centre to the outside of the dish.

Foods such as meat, poultry and thick pieces of fish should be turned over during defrosting, reheating or cooking, and if the oven does not have a turn-table it is advisable to rotate the cooking container to ensure even cooking, especially if the food cannot be stirred.

SHIELDING FOOD

Small smooth pieces of aluminium foil are used to cover small, thin or narrow parts of fish, meat and poultry to slow down their rate of cooking until the thicker, more bulky parts are at least half-cooked. The foil can then be removed.

FOOD ARRANGEMENT

The arrangement of food in the oven is important. For even cooking, food should be at an even height. Spread food level in cooking containers rather than have a mound in the centre. Likewise, when food is ready-plated prior to being reheated, keep food at the same level with the thicker, larger, slower-heating pieces of food around the outside.

Individual foods and small individual cooking dishes should be arranged with spaces in between and preferably in a circle.

Curried Eggs with Green Beans
(page 44)

14

FOODS WITH SHELLS, SKINS, MEMBRANES

Do not attempt to hard-boil eggs in their shells in a microwave oven as the build up of pressure inside the shell will cause them to burst or explode.

Foods with an outer skin or membrane must be pierced to allow steam to escape and prevent bursting. This applies to any fruit or vegetable with a skin as well as egg yolks which should be pierced with the tines of a fork or cocktail stick before placing in the oven.

STANDING TIME

All food continues to cook by heat conduction after it is removed from the oven, and this must be taken into consideration when timing and checking food for readiness. Most foods should be left to stand before serving to allow temperatures to equalise and to complete the defrosting, heating or cooking process. Always underestimate times and check food regularly to prevent overheating or overcooking.

BROWNING

Owing to the speed and moist form of cooking, many foods do not brown in a microwave oven. Larger joints of meat and whole large chickens or turkeys will brown during their longer cooking times. Meat can be brushed with gravy browning, soy sauce or worcestershire sauce to enhance the colour, and cooking meat and poultry in roasting bags encourages browning. Alternatively, you can purchase special microwave seasonings and coatings to sprinkle on meat and poultry before cooking to give them a grilled or roasted appearance. (See also the reference to microwave browning dishes on page 13.)

Important notes

* The recipes and timings given in this book were tested in ovens with maximum power output levels of 600–700W. Only two settings are used and these are referred to as HIGH and LOW (see page 10).
* Most foods are cooked on HIGH, but others which benefit from being cooked more gently at a slower rate are cooked on LOW, which is also the setting used to defrost frozen food.
* The defrosting, heating and cooking times should be used as a helpful guide only and will be affected by several factors which have already been explained. Always underestimate times whether defrosting, reheating or cooking.
* Many foods are covered during cooking. Recipes indicate when this is necessary. If no reference is made to covering, cook the food uncovered.
* The approximate number of servings is given in individual recipes where appropriate.
* Recipe ingredients are given in both metric and imperial measurements. These are not exact conversions, but rather the accepted convenient equivalents. Follow either the metric or imperial quantities, but do not mix the two in any one recipe. In some recipes, metric quantities will give slightly reduced overall volume, but this will not affect the end result, provided you test and check the food at the shortest time recommended for the recipe. It is important to measure ingredients accurately for optimum results.

Defrosting some popular slimmer's convenience foods

Food	Quantity	Approx time on LOW setting	Special instructions	Approx standing time
bacon				
joint	450g (16oz) vacuum pack	6–8 min	slit pack; turn over and rotate during defrosting	10 min
slices	225g (8oz) pack	2–3 min	turn pack over during defrosting	5 min
steaks	2 × 100g (4oz)	3–5 min	separate steaks during defrosting	5 min
bread				
large loaf		6–8 min	unwrap; turn over once or	5–10 min
small loaf		4–6 min	twice	
1 slice	25g (1oz)	10–15 sec	place on kitchen paper; *do not overheat*	1–2 min
bread rolls	2	15–20 sec	place on kitchen paper; *do not overheat*	1–2 min
chicken livers	225g (8oz) carton	3–5 min	turn into a dish; separate during defrosting	3–5 min
crabmeat	225g (8oz)	1¾–2¼ min	turn into a dish; cover	3–5 mins
fruit	225g (8oz)	3–5 min	stir gently during defrosting and	5–10 min
	450g (16oz)	5–8 min	standing	
fruit juice concentrate	178ml (6¼fl oz)	2–3 min	remove collar and lid before defrosting; dilute with cold water	3–5 min
ham, cooked, sliced	100g (4oz) pack	2½–4 min	turn pack over during defrosting	5 min
melbas, trifles	1 individual tub	45–60 sec	remove lid before defrosting	10 min in refrigerator
mousse				
family block		1 min	unwrap before defrosting	2–3 min
individual	1 tub	30 sec	remove lid before defrosting	10 mins in refrigerator
prawns	100g (4oz)	2–2½ min	turn into a dish; cover; stir during	2 min
	225g (8oz)	3½–4 min	defrosting	3 5 min
	450g (16oz)	5 6 min		5 min
sausages (beef)	225g (8oz)	2–3 min	place on a plate; rearrange and turn	5 min
	450g (16oz)	3–4 min	over during defrosting	
smoked mackerel	100g (4oz)	1–2 min	place on a plate; cover	5 min
smoked salmon	85g (3oz) pack	1–1½ min	unwrap, separate slices and place on a plate	1–2 min

Defrosting

Defrosting frozen food must be one of the major benefits of a microwave oven. Most ovens now incorporate a defrost or low setting, but power levels vary between models. The setting used for defrosting in this book is referred to as LOW, giving a power output level of approximately 30–50% (200–300W) on 600–700W ovens. The times given in the chart must be used only as a guide and may vary with the density of the frozen food and the temperature at which it was stored in the freezer, as well as the efficiency of the microwave oven. In addition, food manufacturers sometimes vary product formulas and pack sizes which can alter timing and end results.

HINTS FOR DEFROSTING FROZEN FOOD
1 Always underestimate rather than overestimate defrosting times, especially when defrosting a particular food for the first time.
2 LOW power levels reduce the amount of attention needed, but for best results food should be rearranged, stirred or turned over during defrosting.
3 Food should be rotated during defrosting if the oven does not have a turntable.
4 When frozen food has to be placed in a dish to defrost, match the size and shape of the dish to the size and shape of the food, which should be placed icy-side upwards.
5 Break up frozen blocks gently during defrosting and move the still frozen lumps to the outside of the dish.
6 Remove lids from jars and containers before placing in the oven.
7 As soon as food can be broken up or stirred, cover with clingfilm to retain heat and assist the defrosting process.
8 Open cartons, slit pouches and packages, and flex or shake during defrosting to distribute heat.
9 Remove metal ties from bags and replace with string or elastic bands before placing them in the oven.
10 Fruit should be shaken or stirred gently during defrosting. It should still be icy in the centre when removed from the oven, and should be allowed to stand to thaw completely.
11 When defrosting poultry in its original plastic bag, pour off liquid during defrosting since this absorbs microwave energy and slows thawing.
12 Turn over joints of meat and poultry, separate chops, steaks, bacon slices and rearrange food during defrosting.
13 Do not try to defrost foods completely in the microwave oven, otherwise they may begin to dry or start to cook around the outside edges. The process will finish during standing time.

Timings given in this book were tested in ovens of 600–700W maximum output on full power. Most foods, including those listed in the chart on page 17, were defrosted on LOW setting at an approximate output of 200–300W (ie 30–50% of full power). Times given should be used as a guide only and will vary, depending on the temperature at which the frozen food was stored in the freezer. Check food regularly during defrosting.

Bacon Steaks with Apple Rings (page 70); Chicken à la King (page 74)

Reheating

Foods reheated in the microwave oven taste as good as, sometimes even better than, when freshly cooked. Casseroles, for example, benefit from being cooked one day, cooled and refrigerated overnight and reheated the following day. Using this method, the meat is more tender and flavours have had additional time to mingle and mature. Food for the latecomer can be ready-plated and covered, to be quickly reheated to its original freshness when required, rather than drying up and spoiling as happens with conventional methods of keeping it warm. Food can be cooked in advance of mealtimes and quickly reheated just before serving. This enables the slimmer, who is perhaps cooking different foods for the family, to cook special dishes ready to be reheated at mealtimes.

To save more time, food cooked for the slimmer—and other members of the family—can be frozen in individual portions and reheated in minutes in the microwave oven. This will help to discourage nibbling while waiting for a hot meal.

HINTS FOR REHEATING FOOD
1   Always cover foods which require to be kept moist, and add sauce or gravy to sliced meats before reheating. Thinly sliced meat will heat more evenly than when thickly sliced.
2   Stir casseroles to distribute heat and rotate dishes which cannot be stirred.
3   Underestimate reheating time. Overheating will cause overcooking.
4   Arrange bread and bread rolls on kitchen paper to absorb moisture. Remember, these will be heated in a few seconds, not minutes. Overheating will toughen and spoil bread products.
5   Care is needed when reheating cooked vegetables. Overheated jacket potatoes will dehydrate and fibrous vegetables such as asparagus and broccoli spears will toughen. Vegetables cooked in sauce reheat well.
6   If it is planned to reheat food, slightly undercook it initially.
7   Spread food in an even layer and eliminate mounds, which cause uneven reheating.
8   When a main course is ready-plated before reheating, arrange the food in an even layer with thick or dense foods at the outside and the thinner or quicker-heating foods in the centre of the plate.
9   Feel the bottom of the plate or dish, especially in the centre, during reheating. When the food is hot enough to transfer heat to the plate or dish, it is ready to eat.
10 Food stored in a refrigerator will take longer to reheat than food at room temperature, and food from the freezer will require longest of all.

Timings given in this book for reheating foods were tested in ovens of 600–700W output. Most foods are reheated on HIGH, but others which prefer more gentle heating are reheated on LOW setting. Times given in the chart should be used as a guide only and will vary according to the starting temperature of the food and the efficiency of the microwave oven. Food should be tested for readiness during the reheating period.

Reheating non-frozen cooked foods

Food	Quantity	Approx time on HIGH setting	Special instructions
baked beans, canned	150g (6oz) 220g (7¾oz) 425g (15oz)	¾–1 min 1–1¼ min 1½–2 min	turn into a bowl; cover; stir during heating; stand for 1–2 min
beef, sliced with gravy	1 serving 2 servings 4 servings	1–2 min 2–3 min 3–5 min	place on a plate or in a dish; cover; rotate dish during reheating if oven does not have a turntable
bread rolls (to warm only)	2 rolls 4 rolls	10–15 sec 15–20 sec	place on kitchen paper; *do not overheat*
casserole or stew	1 serving 4 servings	1½–2½ min 10–12 min	cover; stir during reheating
chicken portions	1 × 225g (8oz) 4 × 225g (8oz)	1½–2½ min 6–8 min	cover; rearrange during reheating
custard	250ml (½pt) 500ml (1pt)	2–3 min 3–4 min	stir during reheating
ready-plated main course	1 × 300g (12oz) 1 × 450g (16oz)	2–3 min 3–4 min	cover with clingfilm
soup	250ml (½pt) 1 × 150ml (6fl oz) serving	2–3 min 1¾–2½ min	turn into bowl; cover; stir during reheating
vegetables cooked	100g (4oz) 225g (8oz) 450g (16oz)	½–1 min 1–2 min 1½–2½ min	place in a serving dish; cover; stir during reheating
canned	283g (10oz) 425g (15oz)	1–2 min 2–3 min	turn into serving dish; cover; stir during reheating

Freezer—microwave—table

Many frozen foods, cooked and uncooked, taken straight from the freezer, can be defrosted and reheated or cooked in one operation, without the need to defrost first. This means that a meal can be ready to eat only minutes after its removal from the freezer, and this applies to both home-made and commercially prepared frozen foods. Individual portion packs are particularly beneficial for anyone trying to lose weight since they offer strict portion control, as well as speed and ease of preparation.

USEFUL HINTS
1 Many commercially frozen foods can be placed in the microwave oven in their original bags, pouches or wrappings. Bags and pouches should be pierced or slit to prevent build up of pressure and subsequent bursting and placed on a plate or in a suitable dish.

Low-calorie Soup (page 32); Chicken and Mushroom Casserole (page 105); Baked Apple (page 96)

2 Remove food from foil containers and turn into a suitable dish before placing it in the oven.
3 Match the shape and size of the dish to the shape and size of the frozen food.
4 Stir, shake, rearrange or turn food during the defrosting and reheating or cooking stages.
5 Cover foods which require to be kept moist, such as stews, casseroles and foods in sauce. Foods such as beefburgers and fish fingers are cooked uncovered in the microwave browning dish and turned over after half the cooking time.
6 Always underestimate the overall time required to prevent overcooking.

Times given in the following chart should be used as a guide only and may vary, depending on the temperature at which the frozen food was stored in the freezer. Check food regularly to prevent overcooking.

Frozen foods ready to eat in minutes

Food	Quantity	Approx time on HIGH setting	Special instructions
beefburgers	4 × 50g (2oz)	3–4 min	cook in pre-heated microwave browning dish; turn over during cooking
breaded plaice	1 fillet	3–4 min	cook in pre-heated microwave browning dish; turn over during cooking
casseroles, stews (home-made, cooked)	225g (8oz) meat plus vegetables 450g (16oz) meat plus vegetables	7–10 min 10–15 min	turn into suitable dish; cover; stir during heating
chicken portions, cooked	1kg (2lb)	9–12 min	place in a dish; cover; rearrange during heating
fish cakes	4	3½–4 min	cook in pre-heated microwave browning dish; turn over during cooking
fish fingers	4 10	2½–3 min 3½–4 min	cook in pre-heated microwave browning dish; turn over during cooking
fish in sauce, 'cook-in-bag'	1 × 170g (6oz) bag	6 min on LOW, stand 2 min; further 5 min on LOW	pierce bag; place on plate; cook on LOW setting
fish steaks in breadcrumbs	2	6–7 min	cook in pre-heated microwave browning dish; turn over during cooking
gravy and roast meat	227g (8oz) pack 339g (12oz) pack	8 min 10 min	remove from foil tray; place in similar-sized dish; cover
individual 'cook-in-bag' main course meat dishes	1 × 170g (6oz) bag	5–6 min	slit top of bag; place on a plate; leave to stand 2 min after heating; shake bag gently
kippers	150g (6oz) pack	4–5 min	slit pack; place on a plate; turn over during heating

Food	Quantity	Approx time on HIGH setting	Special instructions
pizza, 17.5–20cm (7–8in)	1	3–5 min	place on a plate or pre-heated microwave browning dish
ready-plated main course	1 × 300g (12oz) 1 × 450g (16oz)	4–5 min 5½–7½ min	cover with clingfilm
quarter-pounders	2 × 100g (4oz)	6 min	cook in pre-heated microwave browning dish; turn over during cooking
sauces	250ml (½pt)	4–5 min	place block in jug or dish; cover; stir during heating; whisk
smoked haddock 'cook-in-bag'	1 × 150g (6oz)	6 min	slit top of bag; place on a plate; stand 2 min after heating; shake gently
soup	250ml (½pt)	4–4½ min	place block in bowl; cover; stir during heating

Slimmer's short cuts

The following ideas will help the slimmer to obtain the maximum use from the microwave oven.

Barbecue owners can partly cook foods without fat in the microwave oven before placing on the grill over the hot coals.

Brie and camembert, the lower-calorie cheeses, can be ripened in seconds on LOW setting.

Cheese spread will spread even further if it is heated, without foil wrapping, for a few seconds in the oven.

Citrus fruits are easier to squeeze and will yield more juice after being warmed for just a few seconds in the oven.

Coffee which has gone cold in your cup or mug need not be thrown away. Reheat it quickly for 1 min or until hot. Similarly, left-over cold percolated or filter coffee can be stored in the refrigerator to be heated as required.

Dry herbs by heating them on kitchen paper until they crumble between the fingers. The exact timing will vary with the herbs. Watch carefully and do not overheat. Check after 30-second intervals.

Fresh peaches are more easily skinned. One peach will require only 15–30 sec in the oven.

Gelatine dissolves in water in seconds without fuss.

Ice cream softens in a few seconds on the lowest setting, making it easier to serve and nicer to eat.

Packet jellies are made up very quickly. Simply cover the cut up cubes with water, microwave for 1½–2 min, stir, and make up with cold water and ice cubes.

Appetisers and hors d'oeuvres

Appetisers and hors d'oeuvres for a meal or cocktail party call for small portions of tasty foods which can be simply and quickly prepared, yet make an impressive start to the occasion. For the slimmer the choice of foods can be especially difficult and many people would find it easier to give up this course rather than the dessert. However, there are times when it is essential to serve a starter, and the following recipes are as low as possible in calories. Some can also be used for lunchtime snacks. With a microwave oven they are all quickly and easily made and a selection of hot hors d'oeuvres, heated as required on a serving plate, will certainly impress your family and guests.

Kipper pâté *(serves 4)*
CALORIES: 680

1 Place kippers, in original pack, on a suitable plate or shallow dish.
2 Use scissors to cut a cross on the top of the pack.
3 Microwave on LOW for about 8 min.
4 Remove skin from fish and place the flesh with the remaining ingredients, except the mustard and cress, into a blender and blend until smooth.
5 Turn mixture into a serving dish or 4 small individual dishes and chill.
6 Serve, garnished with mustard and cress, accompanied by crispbread, toasted low-caloric bread or Melba toast.

1 × 226g (8oz) pack frozen kipper fillets without butter
1 × 226g (8oz) tub low-fat cottage cheese
1 × 15ml tbsp (1 tbsp) lemon juice
dash of anchovy essence or worcestershire sauce
mustard and cress

VARIATION
Substitute frozen smoked mackerel *(colour page 53)* for kipper fillets and replace anchovy essence or worcestershire sauce with 1 × 5ml tsp (1tsp) horseradish sauce.

Slimline cocktail bites *(makes 20)*
CALORIES: 500

1 Wrap each piece of bacon round 1 piece of celery or pepper and secure in position with a wooden cocktail stick.
2 Arrange in a circle on kitchen paper on a plate.
3 Cook on HIGH for about 8–10 min.
4 Dip the ends in paprika before serving.

10 rashers streaky bacon, derinded and cut in half
10 × 2.5cm (1in) lengths of celery
10 × 2.5cm (1in) lengths of red or green pepper
paprika

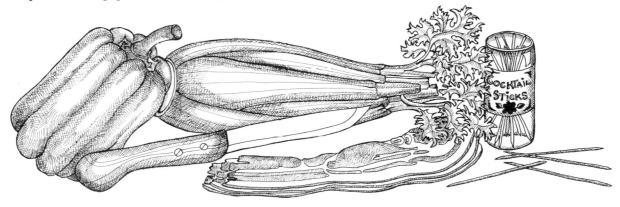

100ml (4fl oz) dry white wine
50ml (2fl oz) soy sauce
garlic salt
12 chicken wings
paprika

Chicken morsels in wine (*makes 24*)

CALORIES: 475

1 Mix together the wine, sauce and garlic salt.
2 Remove and discard wing tips. Remove bones from flesh, dividing each wing in two pieces.
3 Place chicken pieces in a dish, pour over the wine mixture, cover and leave to marinate in refrigerator for at least 2 hours.
4 Remove chicken pieces from marinade and arrange in a single layer in a serving dish.
5 Cover and microwave on HIGH for about 5–7 mins, or until tender. Rearrange during cooking period.
6 Stand for 3 min.
7 Sprinkle with paprika just before serving.

24 dessert prunes
24 salted almonds
8 thin rashers streaky bacon

Devils on horseback (*makes 24*) *colour opposite*

CALORIES: 792

1 Remove stones from prunes and replace with an almond.
2 Derind the bacon and cut each rasher into 3 pieces.
3 Wrap a piece of bacon round each prune.
4 Place in a circle on a serving plate with bacon joins underneath.
5 Microwave on HIGH for about 4 min or until bacon is cooked, rearranging if necessary during the cooking period.
6 Serve speared with cocktail sticks.

225g (8oz) mushrooms, sliced
1 × 15ml tbsp (1tbsp) stock
100ml (4fl oz) natural low-fat yoghurt
1 × 15ml tbsp (1tbsp) low-calorie tomato ketchup
1 × 15ml tbsp (1tbsp) worcestershire sauce
good pinch of dry mustard
1 × 5ml tsp (1tsp) malt vinegar
ground nutmeg
salt and pepper
chopped chives

Hot spiced mushrooms (*serves 3–4*)

CALORIES: 109

1 Place mushrooms and stock in a suitable dish. Cover and microwave on HIGH for about 2 min, stirring after 1 min.
2 Mix together the yoghurt, ketchup, worcestershire sauce, mustard and vinegar. Add nutmeg and seasoning to taste and stir in mushrooms.
3 Spoon the mixture into 3–4 individual dishes and cover each with clingfilm.
4 Arrange the dishes in a circle in the oven and microwave on LOW for about 3 min or until heated. Do not allow the mixture to boil.
5 Sprinkle with chopped chives before serving.

18 prawns, defrosted if frozen
6 rashers streaky bacon

Prawns in bacon (*makes 18*)

CALORIES: 336

1 Derind the bacon and cut each rasher into 3 pieces.
2 Wrap each prawn in a piece of bacon and secure with a wooden cocktail stick.
3 Place on kitchen paper on a plate and cook on HIGH for about 5 min or until bacon is crisp. If liked, cover loosely with kitchen paper to prevent splattering, but do not overcook.

VARIATION
Substitute large shrimp for prawns.

Party Snacks: Devils on Horseback (above); Wrapped Hot Dogs (page 28); Pineapple and Ham Kebabs (page 28)

1 × 425g (15oz) can hot dog
    sausages in brine, drained
8 slices streaky bacon, derinded

Wrapped hot dogs *(makes 16)* *colour page 27*
CALORIES: 1,200

1 Cut each frankfurter in half. Remove any bones from the bacon and cut each slice in half.
2 Wrap a piece of bacon round each frankfurter and secure in position with a wooden cocktail stick.
3 Arrange in a circle on a piece of absorbent kitchen paper on a plate and microwave 8 at a time on HIGH for about 4–5 min or until bacon is cooked.
4 Serve hot.

9 slices thinly sliced lean boiled
    ham
prepared mustard
225g (8oz) thinly sliced edam
    cheese

Dutch ham roll-ups *(makes approx 36)*
CALORIES: 904

1 Spread each slice of ham with a little mustard and top with thinly sliced cheese.
2 Roll up each slice like a swiss roll with the ham on the outside.
3 Cut each roll into 4 pieces and secure with a wooden cocktail stick.
4 Arrange 12 at a time in a circle on a serving plate.
5 Microwave on HIGH for 30–60 sec or until cheese begins to melt. Rearrange during the heating period.
6 Repeat with remaining rolls. Serve hot.

1 × 227g (8oz) can pineapple
    chunks in natural juice or
    water
225g (8oz) cooked ham, cut
    into 1.25cm (½in) cubes
1 × 15ml tbsp (1tbsp) soy sauce

Pineapple and ham kebabs *(makes approx 12)* *colour page 27*
CALORIES: 445

1 Drain the pineapple, reserve juice, and cut each chunk in half.
2 Mix the soy sauce with the reserved juice.
3 Using wooden cocktail sticks, assemble the kebabs with 2 pieces of pineapple at each end and a cube of ham in the middle.
4 Dip each kebab in the mixed soy sauce and pineapple juice before arranging 12 at a time in a circle on a serving plate.
5 Microwave on HIGH for about 1–1½ min, or until heated through.
6 Repeat with remaining kebabs.

2 medium grapefruit
4 × 5ml tsp (4tsp) brown sugar
    or equivalent sugar
    substitute (optional)
cinnamon
2 maraschino cherries, drained
    and halved

Spicy baked grapefruit *(serves 4)* *colour opposite*
CALORIES: 60–160 *(with or without sugar)*

1 Cut each grapefruit in half, remove pips and segment.
2 Sprinkle each half with sugar or sugar substitute, if used, and cinnamon.
3 Arrange in a circle on a plate and microwave on HIGH for about 2½–3½ min.
4 Garnish each with half a cherry before serving.

Spicy Baked Grapefruit (above);
Scrambled Eggs with Chives
(page 105); Tomatoes on Toast
(page 87); Bacon (page 102)

225g (8oz) uniformly sized
   mushrooms
1 × 198g (7oz) can tuna fish in
   brine, drained and flaked
75g (3oz) philadelphia cheese,
   softened
1 × 15ml tbsp (1tbsp) low-
   calorie mayonnaise
1 × 5ml tsp (1tsp) lemon juice
parsley sprigs

Stuffed mushrooms *(makes 12–18)*
CALORIES: 572

1   Remove mushroom stalks and chop finely.
2   Mix together the remaining ingredients, except the parsley sprigs, and
    add the chopped mushroom stalks.
3   Spoon the mixture into the mushroom caps.
4   Arrange 12 at a time in a circle on a serving plate.
5   Microwave on HIGH for 1–2½ min, depending on size. Watch carefully to
    avoid overcooking.

VARIATIONS
Substitute salmon, crab or lobster for tuna fish.

225g (8oz) lean minced beef
½ × 5ml tsp (½tsp) onion salt
pinch of pepper
beaten egg to bind
bottled brown sauce

Cocktail patties *(makes 12)*
CALORIES: 450

1   Mix together the minced beef, salt and pepper and bind together with
    beaten egg.
2   Divide mixture into 12 pieces and form each into patties approx 0.5cm
    (¼in) thick.
3   Lay patties on a plate and brush with brown sauce.
4   Microwave on HIGH for about 1 min.
5   Turn patties over, brush with brown sauce and continue cooking on HIGH
    for about another minute or until medium rare. Cook a little longer if
    preferred well done.
6   Leave to stand for 2 min before serving.

100g (4oz) low-fat cottage
   cheese, sieved
25g (1oz) roquefort
1 × 15ml tbsp (1tbsp) chopped
   walnuts
dash of worcestershire sauce
small round savoury cocktail
   biscuits
paprika

Cheese and walnut canapés *(makes 10–20)*
CALORIES: 346

1   Blend together the cottage cheese, roquefort, walnuts and worcestershire
    sauce.
2   Spread the mixture on the biscuits.
3   Arrange 10 at a time on kitchen paper on a plate and microwave on HIGH
    for 20–30 sec. Watch carefully and do not overheat.
4   Sprinkle with paprika and serve hot.

Cheese puffs *(serves 6 as a starter)*
CALORIES: 395

1 Blend cornflour and milk together in a 500ml (1pt) Pyrex measuring jug.
2 Microwave on HIGH for 30–35 sec or until thick.
3 Beat sauce until smooth.
4 Beat in egg yolks, add cheese, salt, pepper and cayenne.
5 Fold in stiffly beaten egg whites.
6 Half-fill 6–7 individual soufflé dishes or ramekins, capacity 100ml (4fl oz), with the mixture.
7 Arrange the dishes in a circle in the oven and microwave on HIGH for 1–1½ min.
8 Sprinkle lightly with paprika and serve immediately.

1 × 5ml tsp (1tsp) cornflour
50ml (2fl oz) skimmed milk
2 × 55–60g (grade 4) eggs, separated
50g (2oz) mature cheese, grated
salt and pepper
pinch of cayenne pepper
paprika

Cottage cheese and tomato slices *(serves 2–3 as a starter)*
CALORIES: 246

1 Pre-heat a microwave browning dish, following manufacturer's instructions.
2 Spray one side of the tomato slices with low-calorie vegetable oil spray and dip in the crumbs. Place crumb-side down in the pre-heated dish.
3 Spoon cottage cheese on each tomato slice and sprinkle with any remaining crumbs.
4 Microwave on HIGH for about 2 min or until the cheese begins to bubble. Do not overcook.

3 medium firm tomatoes, cut into 1.25cm (½in) slices
3 × 15ml tbsp (3tbsp) crushed cheese-flavoured low-calorie crispbread
175g (6oz) low-fat cottage cheese, plain, or with chives or onion and peppers

VARIATION
Omit cottage cheese, coat both sides of the tomato slices in crumbs and brown on each side. Serve as a vegetable.

Drinks, soups and sauces

Save time by heating drinks in cups or mugs, provided they have no metal trim. Reheat that forgotten half cup or mug of coffee which has gone cold. The slimmer can quickly make a cup or mug of instant black coffee or store percolated or filtered coffee in the refrigerator ready to be heated as required.

A bowl of tasty soup can be warming and nutritious and the basis of a slimmer's meal. When entertaining it can provide a low-fat, low-calorie start to a meal. Use stock cubes dissolved in water when home-made, fat-skimmed stock is not available. When making soup in a microwave oven, choose a container which is large enough to prevent spillage and cover with a lid or plastic wrap. It can, of course, be cooked in the serving dish, and home-made or canned soup can be quickly heated in individual bowls to save washing up.

Sauces add new dimensions to food, but the slimmer must be wary of high-fat, calorie-laden, rich sauces. Reducing or totally eliminating fat, using skimmed milk and calorie-free sweeteners, makes sauces which can be enjoyed by the most ardent slimmer. With a microwave oven sauces are both trouble- and lump-free and ready in a few minutes. They can be measured, mixed and cooked in the sauceboat or serving jug, and should be stirred regularly during cooking. Sample the sauce recipes in this book and you will soon be adapting your own.

Preparing hot beverages
* Hot drinks can be prepared in individual serving glasses, cups or mugs, without metal trim, allowing room for expansion of liquid during heating.
* Microwave, uncovered, on HIGH, but be careful not to allow milky drinks to boil over—these are best heated to serving temperature only.
* Stir liquids before heating, and especially when reheating left-over half cups of tea or coffee. This breaks the surface tension and avoids the likelihood of the liquid 'exploding'.
* When heating more than 2 beverages, arrange them in a circle in the oven for more even heating.

Liquid	Amount	Time on HIGH setting	Amount	Time on HIGH setting
water, milk, or	1 cup	1½–2 min	1 mug	1½–2 min
water and milk,	2 cups	2½–3 min	2 mugs	3–3½ min
for instant	4 cups	4–5 min	4 mugs	6–8 min
coffee, tea,				
cocoa or Bovril				
reheating coffee	1 cup	1–1½ min	1 mug	1½–2 min
or cocoa made	2 cups	2–2½ min	2 mugs	2½–3 min
with milk or	4 cups	3–5 min	4 mugs	5–7 min
water				

Heating canned soups
1 Empty the contents of the can into a soup tureen or individual soup bowls, diluting as instructed if using condensed soups.
2 Cover and microwave on HIGH until serving temperature is reached, noting that some soups should not be boiled. Stir during and after heating.
3 Leave to stand for 1–2 min before serving.

Five-minute Cheesy Chicken Soup (page 35); Cool Cucumber and Prawn Soup (page 35)

32

The following times should be used as a guide when heating canned soups.

Soup	Approx time to heat on HIGH setting
undiluted	
283g (10oz) low calorie	2–3 min
425g (15oz) can	3–4 min
diluted	
298g (10½oz) condensed	4–6 min
1 bowl	2–3 min
2 bowls	3–4 min
4 bowls	6–8 min

Dehydrated packet soup mixes
1 These should be reconstituted according to pack instructions, using a container large enough to prevent spillage.
2 Cover with plastic wrap.
3 Microwave on HIGH until boiling, eg 500–625ml (1–1¼pt), approx 6–8 min; 1 litre (1¾pt), approx 8–10 min.

Chicken stock

1 chicken carcass
850ml (1½pt) boiling water

1 Break up the chicken carcass and place in a large bowl or casserole with the water.
2 Cover and microwave on HIGH for about 15 min.
3 Leave to stand, covered, until cool.
4 Strain and sieve the stock into a bowl.
5 Refrigerate and remove any fat from the surface before use.

VARIATIONS
Meat or ham stock
Substitute meat or ham bones for the chicken carcass and proceed as above.

Mushroom soup *(serves 4)*
CALORIES: 166

1 level 15ml tbsp (1 level tbsp) cornflour
550ml (1pt) chicken stock
275ml (½pt) skimmed milk
salt and pepper
100g (4oz) mushrooms, sliced
1 × 15ml tbsp (1tbsp) lemon juice
finely chopped parsley

1 Blend the cornflour with a little of the measured stock to make a smooth paste. Stir in remaining stock.
2 Pour into a large bowl or soup tureen and microwave on HIGH for 6–8 min or until sauce boils and thickens.
3 Gradually stir in the milk and season to taste.
4 Add the mushrooms, cover and microwave on HIGH for about 3–5 min or until mushrooms are cooked. Stir during cooking.
5 Stir in the lemon juice and sprinkle with chopped parsley before serving.

VARIATION
For a creamier soup, pour into a blender and liquidise before serving, reheating if necessary.

Blushing consommé *(serves 6)*

CALORIES: 195

1 Mix all the ingredients, except sherry, in a large jug or bowl.
2 Cover and microwave on HIGH for about 8–9 min, or until hot but not boiling.
3 Pour into 6 individual soup cups or bowls.
4 Stir 1 × 5 ml tsp (1tsp) dry sherry into each cup or bowl, if used.

1 × 454ml (16fl oz) can tomato juice
1 × 298g (10½oz) can condensed consommé
50ml (2fl oz) lemon juice
1 × 5ml tsp (1tsp) horseradish sauce
2 × 5ml tsp (2tsp) finely chopped parsley
pinch of celery salt
dry sherry (optional)

Five-minute cheesy chicken soup *(serves 4) colour page 33*

CALORIES: 80

1 Pour the stock into 4 individual soup bowls and add the diced cheese, chopped chives and seasoning.
2 Arrange the bowls in a circle in the oven and heat on HIGH for about 5 min, or until hot.
3 Sprinkle with paprika before serving.

550ml (1pt) chicken stock
2 triangles cheese spread, cut into small dice
2 × 15ml tbsp (2tbsp) finely chopped chives
salt and pepper
paprika

Cool cucumber and prawn soup *(serves 4) colour page 33*

CALORIES: 160

1 Pour the stock into a large bowl or casserole.
2 Peel and dice the cucumber and stir into the stock, with the grated onion and seasoning.
3 Cover and cook on HIGH for about 6–8 min, or until the cucumber is soft.
4 Liquidise in a blender or press through a sieve.
5 Allow to cool.
6 Stir in a few drops of green food colouring and then the prawns. Turn into a serving dish or individual soup bowls.
7 Chill well in a refrigerator.
8 Swirl 1 × 15ml tbsp (1tbsp) natural low-fat yoghurt or single cream into each portion before serving.

550ml (1pt) chicken stock
1 large cucumber
1 × 15ml tbsp (1tbsp) grated onion
salt and pepper
few drops of green food colouring
50g (2oz) peeled prawns
4 × 15ml tbsp (4tbsp) natural low-fat yoghurt or single cream

VARIATION
Omit prawns, reserve a few thin slices of cucumber before peeling and float these on top of the soup before serving.

1 medium onion, peeled and
  finely chopped
2 × 15ml tbsp (2tbsp) mixed
  vegetables (sliced carrots,
  sliced runner or french
  beans, peas, broad beans,
  cauliflower sprigs)
850ml (1½pt) boiling chicken
  stock
chopped parsley

Ten-minute vegetable soup *(serves 4)*
CALORIES: 80

1 Place onion and water in a large bowl or casserole.
2 Cover and cook on HIGH for 1–2 min or until soft.
3 Stir in the vegetables and the boiling stock.
4 Cover and cook on HIGH for 8–9 min or until all the vegetables are cooked. Stir after 4 min.
5 Stand, covered, for 2–3 min.
6 Sprinkle with chopped parsley before serving.

2 × 283g (10oz) can low-calorie
  tomato soup
1 × 15ml tbsp (1tbsp) lemon
  juice
2 medium tomatoes, skinned
  and chopped
2 × 15ml tbsp (2tbsp) natural
  low-fat yoghurt
1 × 15ml tbsp (1tbsp) chopped
  chives

Tomato soup *(serves 4)*
CALORIES: 106

1 Mix the soup and lemon juice together in a suitable bowl or jug.
2 Place the chopped tomatoes in the bottom of 4 individual soup cups.
3 Pour the soup over the tomatoes.
4 Cover the cups and arrange in a circle in the oven.
5 Microwave on HIGH for 6–8 min or until heated. Do not allow to boil.
6 Stand for 2 min. Float natural low-fat yoghurt on top of each cup and sprinkle with chopped chives immediately before serving.

350g (12oz) thinly sliced onions
2 × 15ml tbsp (2tbsp) water
850ml (1½pt) boiling beef
  stock
salt and pepper
2 slices low-calorie bread,
  toasted conventionally and
  cut into quarters
50g (2oz) grated edam cheese
cayenne pepper

Dutch onion soup *(serves 4)*
CALORIES: 330

1 Place the onions and water in a suitable dish.
2 Cover and microwave on HIGH for 4–5 min or until onions are soft.
3 Divide the onions among 4 flameproof individual soup bowls and pour in the seasoned boiling stock.
4 Arrange the soup bowls in a circle in the oven and microwave on HIGH for 12–15 min.
5 Float 2 quarters of the toasted bread in each bowl and sprinkle with cheese.
6 Microwave on HIGH for about 2 min to melt the cheese or, if preferred, place the bowls under a pre-heated conventional grill.
7 Sprinkle lightly with cayenne pepper before serving.

Fish with Parsley Sauce (page 38); Chicken with Barbecue Sauce (page 38)

3 medium leeks, washed and
   minced or finely chopped
1 medium onion, peeled and
   minced or finely chopped
225g (½lb) potatoes, peeled
   and finely diced
850ml (1½pt) boiling chicken
   stock
275ml (½pt) skimmed milk
salt and pepper
1 × 142g (5oz) carton natural
   low-fat yoghurt
chopped chives

For pouring
10g (1 level tbsp) cornflour
275ml (½pt) skimmed milk
salt and pepper

For coating
15g (1tbsp) cornflour
275ml (½pt) skimmed milk
salt and pepper

Vichyssoise *(serves 4–6)*
CALORIES: 460

1 Place the leeks, onions and water in a large 2½–3 litre (5–6pt) casserole.
2 Cover and microwave on HIGH for 4–5 min.
3 Add potatoes and boiling stock.
4 Cover and cook on HIGH for about 15 min or until vegetables are cooked. Stir after every 5 min.
5 Sieve or liquidise the soup until smooth.
6 Return the soup to the rinsed casserole and gradually stir in the milk.
7 Cover and cook gently on LOW for about 5 min or until heated through. Do not allow soup to boil.
8 Leave to cool, then refrigerate.
9 Season to taste, stir in yoghurt and sprinkle with chopped chives before serving chilled.

Basic white sauce
CALORIES: 133 *(pouring)*; 166 *(coating)*

1 Blend all ingredients together in a suitable jug or bowl until smooth.
2 Microwave on HIGH for 1 min. Stir well.
3 Microwave again on HIGH for 1 min. Stir well.
4 Continue cooking on HIGH for a further 1–2 min or until sauce has thickened and is cooked. Stir during and at the end of the cooking time.
5 Season to taste and use as required.

VARIATIONS
Parsley sauce (colour page 37)
Add 2 × 15ml (2tbsp) finely chopped parsley to the cooked sauce.

Caper sauce
Add 1–2 × 15ml tbsp (1–2tbsp) drained chopped capers for the final 2 min cooking time.

Cheese sauce
Add 2–3 × 15ml tbsp (2–3tbsp) grated cheese at the end of the cooking time.

Mushroom sauce
Add 100g (4oz) cooked or tinned sliced mushrooms for the final 2 min cooking time.

1 large onion, peeled and finely
   chopped
1 clove garlic, finely chopped
2 × 15ml tbsp (2tbsp) water
2 × 15ml tbsp (2tbsp) malt
   vinegar
2 × 15ml tbsp (2tbsp)
   worcestershire sauce
150ml (5fl oz) tomato purée
150ml (5fl oz) beef stock
2–3 × 5ml tsp (2–3tsp) made
   mustard
salt and pepper

Barbecue sauce *colour page 37*
CALORIES: 145

1 Place the onion, garlic and water in a suitable bowl or jug.
2 Cover and microwave on HIGH for 2½–3 min or until onion is soft.
3 Add the remaining ingredients, blending them well together.
4 Cover and microwave on HIGH for 3–4 min. Stir after 2 min.
5 Stand for 2–3 min before serving with meat, poultry, fish or beefburgers.

Tangy orange sauce

CALORIES: 90

1 Blend all the ingredients well together in a suitable measuring jug.
2 Cover with clingfilm.
3 Microwave on HIGH for about 2–2½ min or until thoroughly heated, stirring after each minute.
4 Stand, covered, for 2–3 min.
5 Stir well before serving with cooked bacon joints, gammon, ham or duck.

2 × 15ml tbsp (2tbsp) low-calorie orange marmalade
2 × 15ml tbsp (2tbsp) distilled or malt vinegar
4 × 15ml tbsp (4tbsp) dry cider
1 × 5ml tsp (1tsp) prepared mustard

Chunky tomato sauce

CALORIES: 75

1 Place the onion and 2 × 15ml tbsp (2tbsp) of the drained tomato juice in a suitable bowl or jug.
2 Cover and microwave on HIGH for 2–3 min or until onion is soft.
3 Add the remaining tomato juice, chopped tomatoes and seasoning.
4 Cover and microwave on HIGH for about 3–5 min. Stir during cooking to prevent sauce spluttering.
5 Leave to stand for 2 min before serving with fish, meat or poultry dishes.

1 large onion, peeled and finely chopped
1 × 397g (14oz) can peeled tomatoes in tomato juice, drained and chopped
salt and pepper

VARIATION
If a smoother sauce is preferred, pour the sauce into a blender to purée before serving.

Savoury egg-based sauce

CALORIES: 130

1 Heat the milk gently in a suitable jug on HIGH for about 1 min until warm, but not steaming.
2 Pour the milk over the beaten egg and mix well together.
3 Microwave on LOW for about 3–3½ min or until sauce has thickened. Stir every ½ min during cooking. Do not overheat or the sauce will curdle.
4 Season to taste and stir well before serving.

1 egg, beaten
150ml (¼pt) skimmed milk
salt and pepper

VARIATIONS
Cheese sauce
Add 25g (1oz) grated cheese and a pinch of mustard with the seasoning.

Parsley sauce
Stir in 1 × 15ml tbsp (1tbsp) chopped parsley before serving.

Caper sauce
Stir in 2 × 5ml tsp (2tsp) capers and a pinch of paprika with salt and pepper to taste.

Seafood sauce
Stir in a few drops of anchovy essence and 15g (½oz) peeled shrimps or prawns.

Sweet sauce
Omit seasoning and flavour sauce with vanilla essence, grated nutmeg, a pinch of ground cinnamon, mixed spice or ginger, or add a little finely grated orange or lemon rind. Artificial sweetener can also be added if found necessary.

1 × 298g (10½oz) can
   mandarins in natural juice,
   drained
2 × 15ml tbsp (2tbsp) cornflour
2 × 15ml tbsp (2tbsp) lemon
   juice
2 × 15ml tbsp (2tbsp) raisins
   (optional)

Mandarin orange sauce

CALORIES: 210

1 Blend cornflour with the mandarin juice until smooth.
2 Microwave on HIGH for about 2–3 min or until sauce has boiled and thickened. Stir after each minute.
3 Add mandarins, lemon juice and raisins, if used.
4 Reheat if necessary on HIGH for ½–1 min.
5 Stir before serving with roast duck or baked ham.

450g (1lb) fresh cranberries
50ml (2fl oz) water
sugar or calorie-free sweetener
   to taste

Cranberry sauce

CALORIES: 64

1 Place the cranberries and water in a suitable dish.
2 Microwave on HIGH for about 4 min or until cranberries pop.
3 Stand, covered, for 5 min. Serve hot or cold with poultry.

2 × 15ml tbsp (2tbsp) custard
   powder
550ml (1pt) skimmed milk
calorie-free sweetener to taste

Custard

CALORIES: 300

1 Blend the custard powder with a little of the measured milk in a suitable measuring jug.
2 Gradually stir in the rest of the milk.
3 Microwave on HIGH for 4 min, stirring after 2 mins.
4 Stir and continue on HIGH for about a further 2–4 min or until custard has thickened, stirring after every 2 min.
5 Add sweetener to taste and stir well before serving.

275ml (½pt) skimmed milk
1 egg, beaten
vanilla essence
calorie-free sweetener to taste

Egg-custard sauce

CALORIES: 180

1 Pour the milk into a suitable jug.
2 Microwave on HIGH for about 2 min until heated.
3 Pour the heated milk over the beaten egg.
4 Strain back into the jug and microwave on HIGH for about 2–2½ min. Do not allow to boil.
5 Add vanilla essence and sweetener to taste, stirring to mix.
6 Use hot or cold as a pouring sauce over fruit and desserts.

275ml (½pt) skimmed milk
15g (½oz) cornflour
2 egg yolks or 1 whole egg,
   beaten
vanilla essence
no-calorie sweetener to taste

Confectioner's custard

CALORIES: 230

1 Blend the cornflour with the egg and a little milk. Gradually add the remaining milk.
2 Cover and microwave on HIGH for 2 min. Whisk well.
3 Re-cover and continue cooking on HIGH for about 1–1½ min or until custard has thickened.
4 Whisk well and add vanilla essence and sweetener to taste.
5 Cover with a piece of wet greaseproof paper to prevent a skin forming, and leave until cold.

Raspberry Wine Jellies (page 91);
Fresh Orange Whip (page 97)

2 egg yolks, beaten
few drops of vanilla essence
1 wineglass dry sherry
no-calorie sweetener to taste

Sabayon sauce

CALORIES: 170

1   Place egg yolks and vanilla essence in a suitable bowl or jug.
2   Microwave on LOW for about 5 min, whisking after every minute until thick.
3   Add sherry and sweetener to taste. Whisk again until mixture is frothy.
4   Stand for a few minutes before serving.
5   Serve either warm or chilled with fruit and desserts.

100ml (4fl oz) water
2 × 5ml tsp (2tsp) arrowroot or cornflour
150ml (6fl oz) natural unsweetened fruit juice
2 × 5ml tsp (2tsp) lemon juice

Fruit sauce

CALORIES: 116

1   Blend the arrowroot or cornflour with the water to give a smooth paste.
2   Gradually add the fruit juices and mix until smooth.
3   Microwave on HIGH for about 3–3½ min or until sauce has thickened and is clear. Stir every minute during cooking.

3 × 15ml tbsp (3tbsp) low-calorie jam
3 × 15ml tbsp (3tbsp) water
2 × 5ml tsp (2tsp) lemon juice

Low-calorie jam sauce

CALORIES: 105

1   Place all the ingredients in a suitable jug or sauceboat.
2   Microwave on HIGH for about 1–1½ min or until jam has just melted. Stir after 45 sec.
3   Stand for 2–3 min before serving.

VARIATION
Low-calorie marmalade sauce
Substitute low-calorie marmalade for jam and proceed as above.

350g (12oz) frozen raspberries or strawberries
2 × 5ml tsp (2tsp) cornflour
1 × 15ml tbsp (1tbsp) lemon juice
red food colouring (optional)

Red berry sauce

CALORIES: 134

1   Place frozen fruit in a suitable dish.
2   Cover and microwave on HIGH for 1–3 min or until slightly icy.
3   Stand, covered, at room temperature until completely defrosted.
4   Drain off the fruit juice and blend with the cornflour in a suitable jug or bowl. Stir in the fruit.
5   Microwave on HIGH for 2–5 min or until thick and clear.
6   Stir in lemon juice and food colouring, if used, and serve hot or cold over ice cream or desserts, or use cold to fill meringue baskets.

VARIATION
Substitute other frozen fruits as preferred.

Eggs and cheese

Eggs

Eggs are invaluable when you are trying to lose weight and with a microwave oven you can prepare a breakfast dish, snack or light main course with incredible speed. They can be baked, poached and scrambled without fat in the oven in minutes—even in seconds in some instances. Eggs are particularly versatile when you are eating alone or are too busy to cook and are tempted by something more fattening such as a sandwich. Don't succumb to this temptation. Cook an egg dish in your microwave oven—it's just as quick, even quicker perhaps, and much more satisfying and nutritious.

Eggs are delicate and cook quickly by any method. When cooked conventionally, the whites start to cook before the yolks, but in a microwave oven the yolks cook first because the microwaves are attracted to the fat in them.

HINTS ON COOKING EGGS
1   Never try to cook eggs in their shells in a microwave oven. The rapid build up of pressure inside the shell will cause the egg to 'explode'.
2   Do not reheat whole, shelled hard-boiled eggs. Halve or slice them first, and cover them with a sauce.
3   Always pierce the yolks of whole eggs with a cocktail stick or prongs of a fork to break the surrounding membrane before baking, poaching or 'frying', otherwise the pressure build up within the yolks during cooking will cause them to burst.
4   Use eggs at room temperature rather than take them straight from the refrigerator.
5   Since eggs cook quickly, it is preferable to cook them slowly on a LOW setting.
6   Scrambled eggs are easiest to cook because the yolks and whites are beaten together, so the cooking pressure is even throughout the mixture. No fat is necessary, and you can mix the eggs with skimmed milk, water, or a mixture of each. Whichever way you choose, the end result will be light and fluffy.
7   Do not overcook eggs and remember that they will continue to cook after they are removed from the oven.
8   Egg-based dishes such as custards and sauces need careful timing to prevent overheating and subsequent curdling.
9   Differences in egg sizes will affect cooking times, so it is always advisable to underestimate this rather than risk overcooking.
10 If you wish to slow down the rate of cooking even more, place a suitable glass or cup filled with water in the oven at the same time as the eggs.
11 Turn dishes which cannot be stirred if the oven does not have a turntable.

Cheese

Cheese must be one of the most deceptive foods for the slimmer. It appears harmless, yet often is high in both calorie and fat content. Hard cheese, and of course cream cheese, are the main culprits, although edam and austrian smoked are preferable to cheddar and other British and continental hard cheeses. Always weigh cheese carefully—it is amazing how much a small piece weighs.

Cottage, quark, ricotta and curd cheeses are the slimmer's friends. They can be used in cooking and served in generous amounts. Brie and camembert are also a good choice, especially for special occasions.

Cheese, like eggs, cooks very quickly in a microwave oven and must be watched and timed carefully to prevent overcooking.

HINTS ON COOKING CHEESE
1 For more even results, always grate cheese whenever possible before cooking.
2 Add cheese towards the end of the cooking time for the final few minutes only.
3 Remove cheese dishes from the oven as soon as the cheese has just melted, otherwise it will be overcooked, tough and leathery, as well as indigestible.
4 Many dishes using cheese are better if cooked on a LOW setting.
5 Undercook rather than risk overcooking cheese dishes.
6 Turn dishes which cannot be stirred if the oven does not have a turntable.

2 stalks celery, finely chopped
1 medium onion, skinned and finely chopped
2 × 15ml tbsp (2tbsp) water
1 small eating apple, peeled, cored and finely chopped
1 × 226g (8oz) carton low-fat cottage cheese, either natural, or with chives, peppers or pineapple
25g (1oz) raisins
1 × level 15ml tbsp (1 level tbsp) tomato purée
2 × 5ml tsp (2tsp) dried parsley flakes
50g (2oz) rolled oats or 100g (4oz) wholemeal breadcrumbs
2 eggs, beaten
dash of tabasco sauce
salt and pepper

Cheese loaf (serves 4)
CALORIES: 570

1 Place the chopped celery, onion and water in a suitable bowl. Cover and microwave on HIGH for 5 min.
2 Stir in apple, re-cover and microwave on HIGH for a further 2 min. Stir.
3 Add the cottage cheese, raisins, tomato purée, parsley flakes and rolled oats or breadcrumbs. Mix well together.
4 Bind the mixture together with the beaten eggs, stir in the tabasco sauce and season to taste.
5 Turn into a loaf-shaped dish, approx 19.5 × 8cm (7½ × 3½in) and microwave on LOW for about 10–15 min or until cooked in the centre. Turn the dish during cooking if the oven does not have a turntable.
6 Leave to cool, then refrigerate.
7 When completely chilled and set, turn out on to a serving platter and garnish with sliced tomato.
8 Serve with salad.

1 × 283g (10oz) can low-calorie chicken or celery soup
1 × 5ml tsp (1tsp) curry powder
4 hard-boiled eggs, sliced
chopped parsley
paprika

Curried eggs (serves 2) colour page 15
CALORIES: 405

1 Combine soup and curry powder in a suitable dish, mixing well together.
2 Cover and microwave on HIGH for 3–4 min or until hot. Stir.
3 Pour over the sliced eggs.
4 Cover and microwave on HIGH for 2–3 min or until heated through. Rotate dish during cooking if the oven does not have a turntable.
5 Serve over cooked green beans, broccoli or bean sprouts. Sprinkle with parsley and paprika.

TV snack for two: Egg and Cheese Ramekins (page 48); Jacket Potatoes (page 89); Fresh Fruit

200ml (8fl oz) boiling water
1 × 5ml tsp (1tsp) vinegar
pinch of salt
2 eggs at room temperature

Poached eggs *(serves 2)*
CALORIES: 160

1 Place the boiling water, vinegar and salt in a 500ml (1pt) round pyrex pie dish or similar suitable dish.
2 Break in the eggs one at a time. Prick the yolks and whites.
3 Cover dish and microwave on HIGH for about 1–1½ min.
4 Leave to stand for 1–2 min to finish cooking before serving. Do not overcook eggs (overcooked yolks will explode).
5 Drain eggs before serving.

How to scramble eggs
The following cooking times should be used as a guide.

Number of eggs	Amount of skimmed milk, water or milk and water mixed	Approx cooking time on HIGH setting
2	2 × 15ml tbsp (2tbsp)	1½ min stirring every 30 sec
3	3 × 15ml tbsp (3tbsp)	2 min stirring every 30 sec
4	4 × 15ml tbsp (4tbsp)	2½ min stirring every 30 sec
6	6 × 15ml tbsp (6tbsp)	3½ min stirring every 30 sec

1 Beat together the eggs, skimmed milk or water and seasoning in a suitable jug or larger bowl, depending on the number of eggs used.
2 Microwave on HIGH for the required time, stirring every 30 sec.
3 Slightly undercook since the eggs will continue to cook after their removal from the oven.
4 Break up with a fork before serving.

4 eggs
4 × 15ml tbsp (4tbsp) skimmed milk
salt and pepper
100g (4oz) peeled shrimps
2–3 slices low-calorie bread, toasted conventionally
parsley sprigs

Shrimp scramble *(serves 2–3)*
CALORIES: 530–565 *(depending on slices of bread used)*

1 Beat the eggs, milk and seasoning together in a suitable dish. Stir in shrimps, reserving a few for garnishing.
2 Microwave on HIGH for 2½–3 min or until egg mixture is just set. Stir after every 30 sec during cooking.
3 Stir well before serving on hot toasted low-calorie bread, garnished with a sprig of parsley.

VARIATION
To serve 4 as a starter, proceed as above but serve on small rounds of hot toasted low-calorie bread, garnished with parsley sprigs and a few shrimps.

2 eggs, preferably at room temperature

Oeufs sur le plat *(serves 2)*
CALORIES: 160

1 Grease 2 saucers or small plates with low-calorie vegetable oil spray.
2 Break an egg on to each and pierce the yolks.
3 Cover with clingfilm and microwave on LOW for about 4–5 min or until egg white is just set. Turn the saucers or plates during cooking if the oven does not have a turntable.
4 Leave to stand for 1–2 min to finish cooking before serving.

Brunch scramble (*serves 3–4*)

CALORIES: 548

1 Place chopped bacon in the bottom of a fairly shallow dish and microwave on HIGH for 2 min. Drain off excess fat.
2 Stir in mushrooms, green and red pepper and microwave on HIGH for a further 2 min. Stir.
3 Beat the eggs and milk or water together lightly in a bowl and stir into the bacon and vegetables.
4 Microwave on HIGH for about 2–3 min, stirring frequently during the cooking period. Increase cooking time if necessary, depending on size of eggs used.
5 Stir well before serving.

VARIATION
Add chopped onions and tomatoes instead of mushrooms and peppers, or use left-over cooked vegetables and cooked ham.

4 slices bacon, chopped
4 × 15ml tbsp (4tbsp) chopped mushrooms
4 × 15ml tbsp (4tbsp) chopped green and red pepper mixed
4 eggs
4 × 15ml tbsp (4tbsp) skimmed milk
salt and pepper

Spanish omelette (*serves 2*)

CALORIES: 429

1 Place the mixed vegetables and potato into a shallow pie plate or dish which has been lightly greased with low-fat spread.
2 Cover and heat on HIGH for 30–45 sec.
3 Beat the eggs and seasoning lightly together and pour over the vegetables.
4 Microwave on LOW for about 8–10 min or until set.
5 Leave to stand for 1 min, but do not fold, before serving.

75–100g (3–4oz) left-over cooked mixed vegetables
1 small cooked potato, diced
low-fat spread
4 eggs
salt and pepper

Eggs mornay (*serves 3–4*)

CALORIES: 830

1 Hard-boil the eggs on a conventional cooker.
2 Meanwhile, make the white sauce in the microwave oven (see page 38). Stir in 50g (2oz) of the cheese.
3 Shell the eggs, cut into slices and arrange them over the base of a shallow flameproof serving dish.
4 Sprinkle the eggs lightly with nutmeg, salt and pepper.
5 Pour the sauce over the eggs and sprinkle the remaining 25g (1oz) cheese on top.
6 Brown under a pre-heated conventional grill and serve.

6 eggs
nutmeg
salt and pepper
275ml (½pt) white coating sauce
75g (3oz) grated cheese, preferably edam

450g (1lb) fresh or frozen
  cauliflower florets
2 × 15ml tbsp (2tbsp) water
2 × 5ml tsp (2tsp) cornflour
275ml (½pt) skimmed milk
salt and pepper
1 × 5ml tsp (1tsp) chopped
  parsley
50g (2oz) grated edam cheese

Cauliflower cheese *(serves 2–3) colour opposite*
CALORIES: 424

1 Place cauliflower with water in a suitable dish.
2 Cover and cook on HIGH for 10–12 min, stirring after 5 min. Leave to stand, covered.
3 Blend cornflour with milk in a jug.
4 Microwave on HIGH for 3–4 min or until sauce has thickened and is cooked. Stir every minute.
5 Add seasoning and parsley.
6 Pour sauce over drained cauliflower and sprinkle with grated cheese.
7 Brown top under a pre-heated grill, if preferred.

scant 10g (½oz) powdered
  gelatine
grated rind and juice of ½
  lemon
2 × 228g (8oz) cartons low-fat
  cottage cheese with
  pineapple
175g (6oz) minced cooked ham
salt and pepper
1 × 15ml tbsp (1tbsp) chopped
  green pepper
1 × 15ml tbsp (1tbsp) chopped
  red pepper
1 × 15ml tbsp (1tbsp) finely
  chopped parsley
thinly sliced cucumber
radish

Cheese and ham loaf *(serves 6–8)*
CALORIES: 630

1 Sprinkle gelatine over lemon juice and leave to soak for a few minutes.
2 Microwave on HIGH for about 30 sec or until gelatine has dissolved. Do not allow to boil. Stir well and leave to cool slightly.
3 When cool, blend into cottage cheese.
4 Stir in ham, lemon rind, seasoning, peppers and parsley.
5 Turn mixture into a loaf-shaped dish and leave to set in refrigerator for at least 1 hour.
6 When completely set, turn out on to a flat serving plate and garnish with the sliced cucumber and radish.
7 Serve, cut in slices, with salad.

2 eggs, at room temperature
2 × 15ml tbsp (2tbsp) grated
  cheese
salt and pepper

Egg and cheese ramekins *(serves 2) colour page 45*
CALORIES: 248

1 Lightly grease 2 ramekins or individual small dishes with low-fat spread.
2 Sprinkle a little cheese in the bottom of each dish.
3 Break the eggs on top of the cheese. Pierce the yolks and whites.
4 Add seasoning and sprinkle with remaining cheese.
5 Cover the dishes and microwave on LOW for about 4–5 min or until eggs are cooked as preferred. Rearrange the dishes during cooking. Do not overcook.
6 Stand, covered, for 1–2 min before serving.

VARIATIONS
Omit cheese and place skinned seasoned chopped tomatoes in the base of each dish before breaking the egg on top.
Omit cheese and place 25g (1oz) chopped lean cooked ham in the base of the dishes, topped with the eggs.

Cauliflower Cheese (above)

170g (6oz) short-cut or shell
  macaroni
550ml (1pt) hot water
1 × 5ml tsp (1tsp) salt
550ml (1pt) skimmed milk or
  macaroni cooking water and
  milk
25g (1oz) cornflour
salt and pepper
½ × 5ml tsp (½tsp) made
  mustard
1 × 5ml tsp (1tsp)
  worcestershire sauce
100g (4oz) grated edam or
  smoked austrian cheese

Macaroni cheese *(serves 4)*

CALORIES: 1,282

1 Place the macaroni, water and salt in a large bowl or casserole, at least 3 litre (5pt) capacity.
2 Stir, cover and cook on HIGH for 6–8 min or until water boils.
3 Reduce setting to LOW and cook for a further 12–15 min or until macaroni is just cooked.
4 Drain, reserving liquid for sauce if preferred, and rinse macaroni in hot water to remove excess starch. Set aside.
5 Blend the cornflour to a smooth paste with a little of the measured liquid, then stir into the remaining liquid in a suitable jug or bowl.
6 Cook on HIGH for 6–8 min or until sauce has thickened. Stir during cooking.
7 Add salt, pepper, mustard, worcestershire sauce and half the cheese.
8 Stir in the macaroni and turn into a 1 litre (2pt) fairly shallow flameproof dish. Sprinkle remaining cheese on top.
9 Microwave on HIGH for about 2–3 min or until reheated.
10 Brown top under a pre-heated conventional grill.

450g (1lb) courgettes, washed,
  trimmed and sliced
25g (1oz) grated parmesan
  cheese
½ × 5ml tsp (½tsp) basil
pinch of salt
15g (½oz) low-fat spread,
  melted

Courgettes parmesan *(serves 4)*

CALORIES: 234

1 Arrange the sliced courgettes in the base of a fairly shallow dish.
2 Mix together the parmesan cheese, basil and salt and sprinkle over the courgettes. Drizzle the melted low-fat spread on top.
3 Cover and microwave on HIGH for about 7–9 min or until the courgettes are crisp but tender.

Fish and seafood

Fish rates highly among the best choice of foods for slimmers. It is high in protein which everyone needs, yet normally low in calories with little or no carbohydrate and fat content. This applies particularly to white fish, most freshwater fish and shellfish which are the ideal choice for anyone trying to lose weight. Oily fish such as herrings, kippers and mackerel are, of course, higher in calories.

There is little risk of becoming bored with fish owing to the wide variety now available fresh, frozen or even canned. When buying fresh fish, do make sure that it is really fresh, especially if you do not live near the coast. In selecting frozen fish, preference should be given to fillets and steaks without a batter or breadcrumb coating, and if you are buying canned fish either select those which are now available canned in brine, or drain thoroughly those canned in oil before use.

With a microwave oven fish takes on a new dimension, especially for the slimmer, because whether fresh or frozen, it can be cooked quickly, without fat, while retaining its delicious flavour. It is the ideal way to cook fish for the results are moist, juicy and tasty. Many owners of a microwave oven who previously ate little or no fish find that it becomes one of their favourite dishes. Cooked in this way, additional sauces or dressings are optional rather than essential, and to enjoy the fish at its best the only necessary accompaniment is a wedge of lemon.

HINTS ON DEFROSTING AND COOKING FISH AND SEAFOOD
1 Frozen fish should be defrosted before cooking.
2 Always cook in a tightly covered dish to retain moisture.
3 *Do not overcook* fish otherwise it will toughen. Test for readiness during the cooking period, remembering that it will continue to cook after its removal from the oven during the standing time.
4 Try to avoid reheating cooked fish, especially small quantities without sauce, since it tends to overcook very easily.
5 Arrange fish in the dish with the thinner parts towards the centre or overlapping and the thicker, fleshier parts towards the outside. Rearrange during cooking if necessary.
6 The tail ends of whole fish can be shielded by wrapping in small pieces of aluminium foil to prevent them overcooking.
7 Large, thick pieces of fish should be turned over after half the cooking time. Cutlets less than 2.5cm (1in) thick need not be turned over, but should be rearranged during cooking.
8 Whole round fish or large cuts with skin on should have the skin scored before cooking to allow steam to escape and prevent bursting.
9 When defrosting frozen fish in the oven, underestimate the time required on LOW setting, otherwise it may start to cook around the outside. Separate fillets, turn whole fish over and stir prawns or shrimps. Allow standing or rest periods during defrosting.
10 Allow fish and seafood to stand at room temperature after defrosting. Rinsing under cold water will complete the defrosting.
11 Rotate the dish during defrosting and cooking if the oven does not have a turntable.
12 Do not attempt to deep-fry fish in a microwave oven—the temperature of the fat or oil cannot be controlled. Besides, if you are trying to lose weight you should avoid all fried foods.

Guide to cooking fresh or defrosted fish

Fish	Weight	Approx cooking time on HIGH setting	Standing time
white fish fillets, steaks, cutlets			
cod, coley, haddock, halibut, plaice, sole, whiting	225g (8oz) 450g (1lb)	2½–3½ min 5–7 min	2 min 2–3 min
smoked fish fillets, cutlets			
cod, haddock, kippers whiting	225g (8oz) 450g (1lb)	2½–3 min 4–5 min	2 min 2–3 min
whole fish	450g (1lb)	6–8 min	2–3 min
salmon, poached	450g (1lb)	4–5 min	3–5 min
scallops	450g (1lb)	4–5 min	2–3 min
lobster tails	450g (1lb)	6–7 min	2 min

Guide to defrosting fish

Fish	Weight	Approx time on LOW setting	Approx standing time
white fish fillets, steaks, cutlets			
cod, coley, haddock, halibut, plaice, sole, whiting	225g (8oz) 450g (1lb)	3–4 min 5–8 min	3–5 min 5 min
smoked fish fillets, cutlets			
cod, haddock, whiting	450g (1lb)	5–8 min	5 min
whole flat fish plaice, sole	450g (1lb)	6–8 min	5 min
whole round fish herring, salmon, trout	450g (1lb)	7–9 min	5–10 min
salmon steaks	450g (1lb)	5–6 min	5 min
scallops	450g (1lb)	5–7 min	3–5 min
shellfish	225g (8oz)	3–5 min	2–3 min
shrimps, prawns	450g (1lb)	5–8 min	3–5 min
lobster tails	450g (1lb)	6–8 min	5 min

Mackerel Pâté with Accompaniments (page 25)

Better results are obtained if fish is allowed to stand for 5 min half-way through the defrosting period.

1 × 198g (7oz) can tuna in
  brine, drained
1 × 340g (12oz) can sweetcorn
  with sweet peppers, drained
1 × 198g (7oz) can sweetcorn
  with sweet peppers, drained
3 eggs
275ml (½pt) skimmed milk
1 level 15ml tbsp (1 level tbsp)
  cornflour
salt and pepper
50g (2oz) grated edam or
  austrian smoked cheese
25g (1oz) low-calorie
  cornflakes, toasted
  conventionally

Tasty corned tuna (*serves 4–5*)
CALORIES: 1,075

1 Break up the drained tuna with a fork and mix thoroughly with the drained corn.
2 Beat together the eggs and milk and blend in the cornflour until smooth.
3 Mix all well together and pour into a 1 litre (2pt) fairly shallow dish.
4 Microwave on LOW for 15 min, rotating dish during cooking if the oven does not have a turntable.
5 Sprinkle with cheese and microwave on LOW for about a further 5 min or until set, rotating dish if necessary.
6 Leave to stand, covered, for 3–4 min before serving sprinkled with the toasted cornflakes.

2 × 15ml tbsp (2tbsp) water
1 small onion, skinned and
  chopped
2 × 15ml tbsp (2tbsp) chopped
  green pepper
75g (3oz) chopped celery
½ level 5ml tsp (½ level tsp)
  basil
salt and pepper
450g (1lb) white fish fillets,
  skinned
1 × 397g (14oz) can peeled
  tomatoes in tomato juice
chopped parsley or chives

Fillets provençale (*serves 3–4*)
CALORIES: 423

1 Place the water, onion, green pepper, celery, basil and seasoning in a suitable dish.
2 Cover and microwave on HIGH for about 4 min or until the vegetables are tender. Drain off liquid.
3 Lay the fish fillets on top of the vegetables with thicker parts towards the outside of the dish.
4 Chop the tomatoes and spoon them with their juice over the fish.
5 Cover dish and microwave on HIGH for about 5–7 min or until the fish is cooked. Rotate dish during cooking if the oven does not have a turntable.
6 Stand, covered, for 3–4 min before serving sprinkled with chopped parsley or chives.

350g (12oz) cod or haddock
  fillets
15g (½oz) cornflour
275ml (½pt) skimmed milk
salt and pepper
1 × 3–4 portion packet
  instant potato
sliced tomato

Fish pie (*serves 3–4*)
CALORIES: 824

1 Arrange the fish in a shallow dish with the thicker parts towards the outside.
2 Cover and microwave on HIGH for about 5 min, turning the dish during cooking if the oven does not have a turntable. Leave to stand, covered.
3 Meanwhile, make a basic white sauce with the cornflour, skimmed milk and seasoning (follow the instructions on page 38).
4 Drain and flake the cooked fish and fold it into the sauce.
5 Turn mixture into a serving dish.
6 Make up the instant potato according to pack instructions, but using water only.
7 Carefully spread the potato over the fish and fork the surface. Top with tomato slices.
8 Microwave on HIGH for about 2 min or until heated through.
9 Brown top under a pre-heated conventional grill, if preferred, before serving.

Fish in french dressing (*serves 3*)
CALORIES: 352

450g (1lb) fish fillets
slimmer's oil-free french
   dressing
lemon wedges

1 Lay the fillets in a shallow dish, pour over a little oil-free dressing and turn the fillets over to coat them in the dressing.
2 Cover and leave to marinate for about 1 hour.
3 Drain the fish and arrange in a shallow serving dish in a single layer with the thicker parts towards the outside.
4 Cover and microwave on HIGH for about 5–7 min or until fish flakes easily.
5 Stand, covered, for 2–3 min before serving with lemon wedges.

Plaice in orange soy sauce (*serves 3*)
CALORIES: 461

450g (1lb) plaice fillets
1 × 15ml tbsp (1tbsp) soy sauce
2 × 15ml tbsp (2tbsp)
   concentrated orange juice,
   thawed
2 × 5ml tsp (2tsp) lemon juice
1 clove garlic, minced or
   finely chopped
orange wedges

1 Arrange the fish fillets in a shallow serving dish with the thicker parts towards the outside.
2 Mix together the remaining ingredients, except the orange wedges. Pour over the fish.
3 Cover dish and microwave on HIGH for 6–8 min or until fish flakes easily.
4 Stand, covered, for 2–3 min before serving garnished with orange wedges.

Haddock portugaise (*serves 4*)
CALORIES: 421

2 medium onions, peeled and
   finely chopped
2 × 15ml tbsp (2tbsp) water
salt and pepper
450g (1lb) haddock fillets
1 × 397g (14oz) can peeled
   tomatoes in tomato juice
finely chopped chives

1 Place onion, water and seasonings in a suitable shallow dish and cover with clingfilm.
2 Microwave on HIGH for 4 min.
3 Arrange the fish fillets on top of the onion with the thicker parts towards the outside.
4 Chop the tomatoes and spoon them, with their juice, over the fish.
5 Cover and microwave on HIGH for about 6–8 min or until the fish flakes easily. Rotate the dish during cooking if the oven does not have a turntable.
6 Stand, covered, for 2–3 min before serving, sprinkled with chopped chives.

2 × 225g (8oz) cod steaks
150ml (¼pt) dry white wine
salt and pepper
diced cucumber
paprika

Cod steaks in white wine *(serves 2)*
CALORIES: 251

1 Place the cod steaks in a shallow round serving dish, just large enough to accommodate the steaks in a single layer.
2 Pour the wine over the fish. Cover and microwave on HIGH for 5–6 min or until fish flakes easily. Turn the dish during cooking if the oven does not have a turntable.
3 Stand, covered, for 2–3 min. Spoon wine over fish.
4 Sprinkle with seasoning, diced cucumber and paprika before serving.

2 × 225g (8oz) cod fillets
1 × 142g (5oz) carton natural low-fat yoghurt
2 × 5ml tsp (2tsp) lemon juice
salt and pepper
25g (1oz) sliced mushrooms
few spring onions, chopped
1 fresh grapefruit, segmented

Citrus cod *(serves 2)*
CALORIES: 285

1 Place the fish in a shallow dish with the thicker parts towards the outside.
2 Cover and microwave on HIGH for 5–6 min. Leave to stand, covered, keeping warm.
3 Meanwhile, mix together the yoghurt, lemon juice and seasoning in a small bowl and microwave on HIGH for 1–1½ min, stirring every 30 sec. Do not allow to boil. Stir.
4 Add the mushrooms and spring onions, stir well and microwave on HIGH for a further minute. Do not allow to boil. Mushrooms should remain firm.
5 Drain the fish, coat with the yoghurt sauce and garnish with grapefruit segments.

4 × 150g (5oz) halibut steaks
salt and pepper
lemon juice
1 lettuce
low-calorie mayonnaise or seafood sauce
1 bunch of watercress
2 small oranges, skin and pith removed

Halibut with orange and watercress salad *(serves 4)*
CALORIES: 448

1 Arrange the steaks in a single layer in a shallow dish.
2 Sprinkle with salt, pepper and lemon juice.
3 Cover and microwave on HIGH for about 6–8 min or until fish is opaque and cooked.
4 Stand for 5 min, then remove cover and leave to cool slightly.
5 Shred a few lettuce leaves and arrange on the base of a shallow serving dish or large oval plate.
6 Place the cooked fish on top and coat with the dressing. Sprinkle the dressing with the grated rind of 1 orange.
7 Garnish with watercress and the sliced or segmented oranges.

450g (1lb) sole fillets
2 × 5ml tsp (2tsp) cornflour
7 × 15ml tbsp (7tbsp) skimmed milk
salt and pepper
1 × 15ml tbsp (1tbsp) chopped parsley
1 bay leaf

Plaice with Prawn Sauce (page 59); Fillets of Sole in Parsley Sauce (above)

Fillets of sole in parsley sauce *(serves 3–4)* *colour opposite*
CALORIES: 432

1 Place the fillets in a shallow dish with the thicker edges towards the outside.
2 In a small bowl, blend the cornflour and milk together until smooth. Stir in the salt, pepper, parsley and bay leaf.
3 Pour the cornflour mixture over the fish.
4 Cover and microwave on HIGH for 4 min.
5 Baste the fish with the sauce, re-cover and microwave on HIGH for a further 2–3 min or until the fish flakes easily.
6 Stand, covered, for 2–3 min.
7 Remove bay leaf and spoon sauce over fish before serving.

450g (1lb) white fish fillets, fresh or defrosted
lemon juice
salt and pepper
50g (2oz) toasted flaked almonds
lemon slices or wedges

Fillets almondine (serves 4)
CALORIES: 552

1 Arrange fish in a single layer in a shallow dish with the thickest parts towards the outside.
2 Sprinkle with lemon juice and seasoning.
3 Cover and cook on HIGH for 5–6 min or until fish is opaque. Turn the dish after 2½ min if the oven does not have a turntable.
4 Leave to stand for 2 min before serving sprinkled with the almonds and garnished with lemon slices or wedges.

4 large tomatoes
1 × 213g (7½oz) can tuna in brine, drained and flaked
1 × 15ml tbsp (1tbsp) lemon juice
1 × 15ml tbsp (1tbsp) diced cucumber
25g (1oz) grated mature cheese
freshly ground black pepper
cucumber twists

Tuna and cheese stuffed tomatoes (serves 4) colour page 61
CALORIES: 348

1 Cut the tops off the tomatoes and scoop out the flesh.
2 Mix the flesh with the remaining ingredients, except the cucumber twists.
3 Fill the tomatoes with the mixture and arrange them in a circle on a plate or in a shallow round dish.
4 Cover with clingfilm and microwave on HIGH for about 3 min or until filling is heated. Turn the dish during the heating period if the oven does not have a turntable.
5 Leave to stand for 2 min.
6 Garnish with cucumber twists before serving with salad.

2 × 225g (8oz) cod steaks
salt and pepper
lemon juice
2 × 15ml tbsp (2tbsp) diced cucumber
50g (2oz) thinly sliced mushrooms
1 × 142g (5oz) carton natural low-fat yoghurt
paprika
sprigs of parsley

Cod steaks with cucumber and mushroom dressing (serves 2)
CALORIES: 228

1 Arrange cod steaks in a single layer in a suitable shallow serving dish.
2 Sprinkle with salt, pepper and lemon juice.
3 Cover with clingfilm and cook on HIGH for 3 min.
4 Turn fish over and continue to cook, covered, on HIGH for a further 3–4 min or until cooked.
5 Leave to stand, covered, while preparing the dressing.
6 Fold the cucumber and mushrooms into the yoghurt.
7 Spoon this mixture over the fish, cover and heat on HIGH for about 2 min. Do not allow to boil.
8 Leave to stand for 2–3 min before serving sprinkled lightly with paprika and garnished with parsley sprigs.

1 medium onion, peeled and finely chopped
2 × 15ml tbsp (2tbsp) finely chopped celery
2 × 15ml tbsp (2tbsp) chopped green pepper
2 × 15ml tbsp (2tbsp) water
salt and pepper
pinch of basil
450g (1lb) white fish fillets
1 × 298g (10½oz) can condensed golden vegetable soup

Fish casserole (serves 4)
CALORIES: 502

1 Place the onion, celery, green pepper and water in a shallow dish measuring 25 × 15cm (10 × 6in).
2 Cover and microwave on HIGH for 2–3 min or until the onion is partly cooked.
3 Stir in salt, pepper and basil.
4 Arrange the fish in the dish with the thicker edges towards the outside.
5 Spoon the soup over the fillets and cover the dish with clingfilm.
6 Microwave on HIGH for about 7–9 min or until the fish flakes easily.
7 Stand, covered, for 3–5 min before serving.

Plaice with prawn sauce *(serves 3–4)* *colour page 57*

CALORIES: 538

450g (1lb) plaice fillets,
1 × 142g (5oz) carton natural low-fat yoghurt
2 × 5ml tsp (2tsp) low-calorie tomato sauce
1 × 5ml tsp (1tsp) tomato purée
dash of worcestershire sauce
salt and pepper
1 × 92g (3½oz) can peeled prawns, drained
lemon wedges

1 Arrange fish in a shallow dish with thicker parts towards the outside.
2 Cover and microwave on HIGH for about 5–7 min or until fish flakes easily. Turn the dish during cooking if the oven does not have a turntable.
3 Leave to stand, covered.
4 Meanwhile, mix together the yoghurt, tomato sauce, tomato purée and worcestershire sauce. Season to taste and add most of the prawns, reserving a few to garnish.
5 Heat the sauce on HIGH for 1–1½ min or until hot but not boiling. Stir during cooking.
6 Pour the sauce over the cooked fish and garnish with reserved prawns. Serve with lemon wedges.

VARIATION

Substitute other white fish for plaice and use shrimps instead of prawns, eg cod with shrimp sauce.

Juicy salmon steaks *(serves 4)*

CALORIES: 1,440

4 salmon steaks, 2.5cm (1in) thick, weighing about 1kg (2–2½lb)
8 × 15ml tbsp (8tbsp) water
1 × 15ml tbsp (1tbsp) lemon juice
1 × 15ml tbsp (1tbsp) finely chopped lemon rind
salt and pepper
lemon wedges
cress
cucumber salad (optional)

1 Arrange the steaks in a single layer in a suitable shallow dish.
2 Mix together the water, lemon juice, lemon rind and seasoning and pour over the fish.
3 Cover the dish with clingfilm and cook on HIGH for 4 min.
4 Turn steaks over and cook on HIGH for about a further 3–5 min or until the flesh is opaque in the centre and can be separated easily from the bone.
5 Leave to stand, covered, for 5 min.
6 Arrange the cooked steaks on a heated serving plate or dish.
7 Spoon the strained cooking liquor over them and garnish with lemon wedges and cress.
8 If liked, serve with cucumber salad.

CUCUMBER SALAD

Fold thinly sliced cucumber through natural yoghurt. Turn into a serving dish lined with crisp lettuce leaves and sprinkle with paprika.

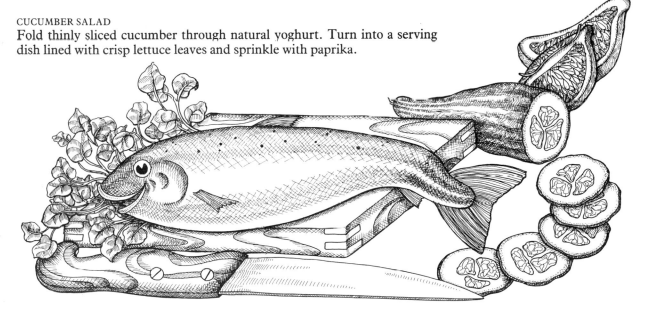

175–225g (6–8oz) turbot,
defrosted if frozen
1 × 15ml tbsp (1tbsp) diced
green pepper
1 × 15ml tbsp (1tbsp) diced
red pepper
1 × 15ml tbsp (1tbsp) lemon
juice
low-calorie seafood sauce
salt, freshly ground black
pepper
100g (4oz) peeled prawns
watercress, lettuce or shredded
chinese leaves
black olives
lemon twists or wedges

Scalloped turbot with prawns (serves 4)
CALORIES: 336–338 (depending on weight of turbot)

1 Lay fish on a suitable plate and cover with clingfilm.
2 Cook on HIGH for about 3 min or until firm but opaque and cooked. If thick, turn the fish over during cooking.
3 Leave to stand, covered, until cold, then cut into cubes.
4 Meanwhile, mix together the green and red pepper, lemon juice, seafood sauce and seasoning to taste.
5 Fold in the cold cubed turbot and most of the prawns.
6 Line 4 scallop shells with watercress, lettuce or chinese leaves.
7 Pile the fish mixture on top.
8 Garnish with reserved prawns, black olives and lemon twists or wedges.

VARIATIONS
Substitute cod, haddock or halibut for turbot. Use shrimps instead of prawns.

25g (1oz) low-fat spread
2 × 15ml tbsp (2tbsp) finely
chopped parsley
pinch of mixed herbs
salt and pepper
4 plaice fillets, skinned
1 × 5ml tsp (1tsp) cornflour
3 × 15ml tbsp (3tbsp) water
grated rind and juice of
½ lemon

Plaice roll-ups (serves 2)
CALORIES: 546

1 Mix together the low-fat spread, parsley, herbs and seasoning.
2 Lay the fillets skinned-side uppermost and spread with the mixture.
3 Roll up firmly and place in a shallow dish just large enough to hold them in a single layer.
4 Cover and cook on HIGH for about 4 min. Leave to stand, covered.
5 Meanwhile, blend the cornflour with the water, lemon rind and juice in a suitable small bowl.
6 Microwave on HIGH for about 1½ min or until sauce is cooked. Stir during cooking. Season to taste.
7 Pour the sauce over the cooked fish and reheat if necessary on HIGH for about 1 min.
8 Cut the remaining half lemon into wedges to serve with the fish.

4 herrings, cleaned and boned
salt and pepper
1 onion, peeled and thinly
sliced
6 peppercorns
1–2 bay leaves
150ml (¼pt) malt vinegar
150ml (¼pt) water

Soused herrings (serves 4) colour opposite
CALORIES: 705

1 Remove heads, tails and fins from fish and sprinkle flesh with salt and pepper.
2 Roll up from head to tail and secure with wooden cocktail sticks.
3 Pack into a fairly shallow dish in a single layer.
4 Add the onion, peppercorns and bay leaves and pour over the vinegar and water.
5 Cover and cook on HIGH for about 6–7 min rotating the dish after about 3 min if the oven does not have a turntable.
6 Leave to cool in the cooking liquid. Refrigerate before removing cocktail sticks, serving as an appetiser or with salad.

Note If preferred, the tails can be left on and when the rolled fish are placed in the dish, arrange the tails pointing upwards.

Soused Herrings (above); Tuna and Cheese Stuffed Tomatoes (page 58)

450g (1lb) sole fillets
2 × 5ml tsp (2tsp) horseradish
  sauce
2 × 5ml tsp (2tsp) dijon
  mustard
1 × 15ml tbsp (1tbsp) lemon
  juice
2 × 15ml tbsp (2tbsp) grated
  edam cheese
75ml (3fl oz) natural low-fat
  yoghurt

Sole supreme *(serves 3–4)*

CALORIES: 517

1 Arrange the fillets in a single layer in a shallow dish.
2 Mix together the remaining ingredients and spread evenly over the fish.
3 Cover with clingfilm and cook on HIGH for about 6–8 min or until the flesh flakes easily when tested with a fork. Rotate the dish during cooking if the oven does not have a turntable.
4 Leave to stand, covered, for 2–3 min before serving.

675g (1½lb) scallops
50ml (2fl oz) vegetable oil
1 × 15ml tbsp (1tbsp) lemon
  juice
pinch of basil
pinch of rosemary
salt and pepper
1 lemon, thinly sliced
paprika

Marinated scallops *(serves 4–6)*

CALORIES: 960

1 Rinse the scallops in water and pat dry with kitchen paper.
2 If large, cut the scallops in half before placing in a bowl or dish.
3 Combine the remaining ingredients, except the paprika, and pour over the scallops.
4 Stir well to mix and coat the scallops with the marinade.
5 Cover and leave to marinate in the refrigerator for at least 2 hours.
6 Remove the scallops from the marinade and place in a suitable serving dish. Reserve the lemon slices.
7 Cover and microwave on HIGH for about 7–9 min, rearranging the scallops and adding the lemon slices after 4 min.
8 Stand, covered, for a few minutes before serving, sprinkled with paprika.

Meat and poultry

Everyone needs a regular supply of protein, most of which is obtained from meat, poultry and fish. When trying to lose weight and at the same time remain healthy, a good supply of protein can compensate for a reduction in fat and carbohydrate, but nothing can replace protein.

Protein foods are satisfying foods, but unfortunately many red meats are deceptively high in calories. For this reason, meat for the slimmer should be as lean as possible, with all visible fat removed before cooking. It should then be cooked without fat and drained of fat drawn out during cooking before serving. Portions should be carefully weighed. Offal, such as liver and kidney, are lower in calories and rich in vitamins and minerals. Indeed, when you are trying to lose weight, the inclusion of liver with its high iron content in your diet, at least once a week, is a healthy practice.

Poultry is lower in calories and fat content than most red meats, especially when the skin is removed before eating. It is easily digested, economical and versatile and can be cooked and presented in many different ways. The carcass, with the addition of vegetables, can be used to make nutritious stock to form the basis of tasty low-calorie soups and sauces.

In a microwave oven meat and poultry can be roasted without fat. Joints of meat and poultry cooked in a pierced roasting bag in the oven are tender, moist and juicy and consequently full of flavour. The prime cuts of meat do not require any special treatment, but cheaper, less tender cuts are best marinated before cooking, and cooked in the oven on LOW setting to slow down the speed of microwave cooking sufficiently to allow the meat to tenderise and flavours to develop and mingle, such as in stews and casseroles. In fact, when making stews or casseroles best results are obtained if they are cooked the day before, cooled, refrigerated overnight, and gently reheated on LOW setting when required the following day.

Poultry presents no problems, and the fact that the skin does not become as crisp as when cooked conventionally will not interest the slimmer since it will not be eaten.

HINTS ON DEFROSTING AND COOKING MEAT AND POULTRY
1   Both meat and poultry should be thoroughly defrosted before cooking and should preferably be at room temperature rather than taken straight from the refrigerator.
2   If they are to be defrosted in the microwave oven they should be placed in their original wrappings in a dish to catch the juices, removed while still icy in the centre and left to defrost completely during the standing time. Remember to remove the giblets from poultry after defrosting and before cooking.
3   Joints of meat and whole poultry are best cooked in pierced roasting bags on a microwave roasting rack or upturned saucer and should be turned over after half the cooking time.
4   Poultry should be well trussed to give an even shape and to keep the wings and legs close to the body.
5   Joints of meat of regular shape will cook more evenly than awkward shapes.
6   Shield narrow ends of awkward-shaped joints and the wing and leg tips of poultry with small pieces of foil to prevent overcooking.
7   Drain off excess juices during roasting, refrigerate, skim off fat and use for unthickened gravy or in sauces.
8   Arrange chicken portions in a single layer with the thinner, narrow ends

Stuffed Meat Roll (page 67)

towards the centre of the dish and the thicker, more fleshy parts towards the outside.

9 Stir stews and casseroles during cooking and rotate the dish if the oven does not have a turntable.

10 Cut meat and vegetables for stews and casseroles into even-sized pieces for more even cooking.

11 Use a meat thermometer to determine whether joints of meat and whole poultry are thoroughly cooked. Use only special microwave meat thermometers inside the microwave oven.

12 Allow meat and poultry to stand after cooking to allow heat to equalise and internal temperature to rise.

Guide to defrosting meat and poultry

Food	Weight	Approx time on LOW setting	Special instructions	Approx standing time
MEAT joints: beef, lamb, veal, pork	up to 2kg (4lb)	8–10 min per 450g (1lb)	turn over during defrosting; shield any warm parts with small pieces of foil	30–60 min
minced meat	450g (1lb)	8–10 min	break down during defrosting	5–10 min
steak, cubed	450g (1lb)	8–10 min	rearrange during defrosting	10 min
chops	450g (1lb)	6–8 min	rearrange during defrosting	10–15 min
liver, kidney	450g (1lb)	6–9 min	separate during defrosting	5 min
sausages/ sausagemeat	450g (1lb)	6–7 min	separate sausages, break down sausagemeat during defrosting	5–10 min
steak, rump, sirloin	450g (1lb)	8–10 min	turn over during defrosting	10 min
POULTRY chicken whole	per 450g (1lb)	6–8 min	thaw in original wrapping; turn over during defrosting	30 min in cold water; remove giblets
portions	450g (1lb)	7–10 min	turn over during defrosting	10 min
duckling	per 450g (1lb)	6–8 min	thaw in original wrapping; turn over and rest during defrosting	30–40 min in cold water; remove giblets
BACON joint	450g (1lb) vacuum pack	6–8 min	slit pack; turn over and rotate during defrosting	10 min
slices	225g (8oz)	2–3 min	turn pack over during defrosting	5 min
steaks	2 × 100g (4oz)	3–5 min	separate steaks during defrosting	5 min

Guide to roasting meat and poultry

Food	Approx time per 450g (1lb) on HIGH setting	Internal temp before standing	Approx standing time
beef joint			
rare	6–7 min	55°C (130°F)	10–15 min
medium	7–8 min	65°C (150°F)	10–15 min
well done	8½–10 min	70°C (160°F)	15–20 min
lamb joint	8–10 min	82°–85°C (180°–185°F)	15–20 min
veal joint	8½–9 min	70°C (160°F)	15–20 min
pork joint	9–10 min	85°C (180°F)	20–25 min
chicken			
whole	6–8 min	82°–85°C (180°–185°F)	10–15 min
portions	6–9 min		10 min
duckling	6–8 min	82°–85°C (180°–185°F)	10–15 min
turkey ★	6–8 min	82°–85°C (180°–185°F)	15–20 min

★ Better results are obtained if turkey is cooked for only half the time on full power, and then cooked at a lower setting—(see individual oven manufacturer's instructions for maximum weights and cooking procedure recommended)

Guide to cooking bacon slices
★ Bacon should always be cooked in a single layer, either on a special microwave roasting rack covered with absorbent kitchen paper to prevent splashing, or on a plate sandwiched between double thicknesses of absorbent kitchen paper.
★ Snip the rind and fat at regular intervals with kitchen scissors before cooking to prevent bacon curling up during cooking.
★ Pour off excess fat during cooking.
★ At the end of the cooking period remove the paper immediately to prevent sticking.

No of slices	Approx cooking time on HIGH setting
2	2–2½ min
4	4–4½ min
6	5–6 min

Smothered lamb chops *(serves 4)* *colour page 73*
CALORIES: 856

1 Arrange chops in a single layer in a suitable dish and sprinkle with onion and garlic.
2 Cover and microwave on HIGH for 5 min. Turn the chops over and spoon the onion and garlic on top.
3 Mix together the remaining ingredients and spoon over the chops.
4 Cover and cook on LOW for about 12–15 min or until chops are tender. Rearrange chops in the dish after about 6 min.
5 Stand, covered, for 5 min before serving.

4 lamb chops
1 medium onion, coarsely chopped
1 clove garlic, finely chopped
100ml (4fl oz) tomato purée
4 × 5ml tsp (4tsp) worcestershire sauce
1 × 5ml tsp (1tsp) prepared mustard

Stuffed meat roll *(serves 6)* *colour page 65*
CALORIES: 1,305

1 In a large bowl mix together the minced beef, breadcrumbs, worcestershire sauce and seasoning. Bind together with a beaten egg.
2 Turn the mixture out on to a large piece of greaseproof paper or plastic wrap and pat it out to form a rectangle 1.25cm (½in) thick.
3 Sprinkle the meat with the chopped vegetables, leaving a 2.5cm (1in) border uncovered on all sides.
4 Roll up, swiss-roll style, using the greaseproof paper or plastic wrap to help the rolling, peeling it back to keep it free.
5 Place the roll with seam underneath in a suitable dish.
6 Microwave on HIGH for 10 min, turning the dish after 5 min if the oven does not have a turntable.
7 Reduce setting to LOW and continue cooking for a further 20–30 min or until meat is cooked as preferred.
8 Leave to stand for 5 min before serving. Serve either hot or cold.

675g (1½lb) lean minced beef
2 × 15ml tbsp (2tbsp) low-calorie breadcrumbs
1 × 5ml tsp (1tsp) worcestershire sauce
salt and pepper
2 eggs, beaten
1 green pepper, deseeded and chopped finely
2 × 15ml tbsp (2tbsp) finely chopped red pepper
1 medium onion, peeled and chopped

VARIATION
Meat loaf
Omit the green and red pepper. Mix together the remaining ingredients and turn into a loaf-shaped dish approx 20 × 12.5cm (8 × 5in).
Microwave on HIGH for about 20 min or until the internal temperature in the centre of the meat loaf is 77°–80°C (170°–175°F). Rotate the dish during cooking if the oven does not have a turntable. If the meat loaf is preferred slightly underdone in the centre, reduce the cooking time by about 4 min.

Beef ring cluster *(serves 6)*
CALORIES: 1,360

1 Mix together in a bowl the beef, breadcrumbs, onion, mustard, worcestershire sauce and seasoning. Bind together with beaten egg.
2 With wetted hands, divide the mixture into 6 equal portions and roll into large balls.
3 Place the balls close together in a suitable ring mould. If a ring mould is not available, place a glass jar in the centre of a 1.7 litre (3pt) casserole and pack the balls around the outside.
4 Flatten the balls slightly to level the top surface.
5 Brush the top with the tomato sauce.
6 Microwave on HIGH for 10–15 min or until meat is cooked as preferred. Turn the dish every 5 min if the oven does not have a turntable.
7 Leave to stand for 5–10 min before serving.

675g (1½lb) lean minced beef
2 × 15ml tbsp (2tbsp) low-calorie breadcrumbs
1 medium onion, finely chopped
½ × 5ml tsp (½tsp) dry mustard
dash of worcestershire sauce
salt and pepper
2 eggs, beaten
2 × 15ml tbsp (2tbsp) low-calorie tomato sauce

450g (1lb) lean minced beef
2 medium onions, peeled and
finely chopped
1 × 397g (14oz) can peeled
tomatoes in tomato juice
2 × 15ml tbsp (2tbsp) tomato
purée
salt and pepper
2–4 × 5ml tsp (2–4tsp) chilli
powder, according to taste
1 × 425g (15oz) can red kidney
beans, drained

Chilli con carne *(serves 4)* *colour opposite*
CALORIES: 1,085

1 Break up the meat with a fork and place in a suitable dish.
2 Microwave on HIGH for 4 min. Drain off fat.
3 Break up the meat again with a fork, stir in the chopped onion and microwave on HIGH for a further 3–4 min or until the meat is no longer pink. Drain off fat.
4 Add the tomatoes with their juice, tomato purée, salt, pepper and chilli powder to taste.
5 Cover and cook on LOW for 25 min.
6 Add drained kidney beans, stirring well to mix.
7 Cover and continue cooking on LOW for a further 20–25 min.
8 Stand for 2–3 min before serving.

1 medium onion, peeled and
chopped
450g (1lb) pig's liver, skinned
and sliced
6 slices streaky bacon,
derinded, cut in half and
rolled
1 × 397g (14oz) can peeled
tomatoes in tomato juice
2 × 15ml tbsp (2tbsp) tomato
purée
salt and pepper

Liver, bacon and tomato casserole *(serves 4)*
CALORIES: 799

1 Place the chopped onion with 15ml (1tbsp) water in a casserole.
2 Cover and cook on HIGH for 1½ min.
3 Remove any tubes from the liver before adding to the casserole with the remaining ingredients, arranging the bacon rolls on top.
4 Cover and cook on HIGH to bring to the boil, then reduce to LOW and cook for a further 20–25 min.
5 Leave to stand for 5 min before serving.

4 pork loin chops, trimmed
1 medium onion, peeled and
finely chopped
4 × 15ml tbsp (4tbsp) tomato
purée
1 × 15ml tbsp (1tbsp) soy sauce
3 × 5ml tsp (3tsp) malt vinegar
1 × 226g (8oz) can pineapple
rings in natural juice, drained
and diced

Sweet and sour pork chops *(serves 4)*
CALORIES: 1,625

1 Arrange chops in a single layer in a suitable dish.
2 Mix together the tomato purée, soy sauce and vinegar. Stir in the pineapple juice, diced pineapple and onions.
3 Spoon the mixture over the chops.
4 Cover and cook on HIGH for 6–8 min.
5 Turn chops over, re-cover and continue cooking on HIGH for a further 6–8 min or until fork tender.
6 Leave to stand, covered, for 5 min before serving.

Chilli Con Carne (above)

1 medium cabbage
2 × 15ml tbsp (2tbsp) water
1 × 425g (15oz) can lean
   minced beef with onions
275ml (½pt) tomato juice
seasoning

Stuffed cabbage rolls *(serves 4)*
CALORIES: 976

1 Discard the tough outer cabbage leaves and select 8 large perfect leaves. Use the remaining cabbage for another meal.
2 Remove the hard centre rib and place the leaves with the water in a large bowl.
3 Cover and microwave on HIGH for about 5 min or until soft. Drain.
4 Turn the contents of the can of meat into a bowl and mix well together.
5 Spread a generous portion of the mixture in the centre of each cabbage leaf.
6 Fold the sides of the leaves over and roll them up firmly.
7 Place in a single layer, seam-side down, in a suitable dish. Pour the seasoned tomato juice over the rolls.
8 Cover and cook on HIGH for 3 min, then continue on LOW for about a further 5–8 min or until filling is hot and cabbage is tender. Turn the dish during cooking if the oven does not have a turntable.

450g (1lb) lean minced beef
1 medium onion, peeled and
   finely chopped
1 garlic clove, minced or finely
   chopped
2 × 15ml tbsp (2tbsp) tomato
   purée
1 × 397g (14oz) can peeled
   tomatoes in tomato juice
1 × 5ml tsp (1tsp) dried herbs
150ml (5fl oz) boiling beef stock
salt and pepper

Bolognese sauce *(serves 4–6)*
CALORIES: 785

1 Crumble mince and combine with the onion and garlic in a suitable dish.
2 Cover and cook on HIGH for 5 min.
3 Drain off fat and break up mince with a fork. Mix well.
4 Add the tomato purée, chopped tomatoes with their juice, herbs, stock and seasoning.
5 Cover and cook on HIGH for about 15 min, stirring during the cooking period.
6 Stand for 5 min before serving over heated fresh or canned bean sprouts rather than cooked spaghetti.

4 lean picnic steaks, each
   weighing about 100g (4oz)
1 large dessert apple,
   unskinned
lemon juice
ground cinnamon (optional)

Bacon steaks with apple rings *(serves 4)* colour page 19
CALORIES: 540

1 Arrange the steaks in a dish in a single layer.
2 Core the unskinned apple and cut into 4 slices. Sprinkle with lemon juice.
3 Lay a slice of apple on each steak and sprinkle with a little cinnamon, if used.
4 Cover and cook on HIGH for about 5–6 min or until tender. Turn the dish during cooking if the oven does not have a turntable.
5 Leave to stand, covered, for 2–3 min before serving.

Five-minute shepherd's pie (*serves 3–4*)

CALORIES: 856

1 Turn the meat into a suitable dish and spread evenly over the base. Sprinkle with worcestershire sauce.
2 Make up the instant potato according to pack instructions, but using water only.
3 Spread the potato over the meat and draw the prongs of a fork over the top surface to decorate.
4 Microwave on HIGH for about 4–5 min or until heated through. Rotate the dish during heating if the oven does not have a turntable.
5 Brown top, garnished with tomato slices, under a pre-heated conventional grill.
6 Serve hot with green vegetables.

1 × 439g (15½oz) can minced beef with onions
worcestershire sauce
1 × 3–4 portion packet instant potato
2 tomatoes

Meatball and cabbage casserole (*serves 4*)

CALORIES: 896

1 Arrange the cabbage in the base of a fairly shallow square or oblong dish. Pour stock over the cabbage.
2 Cover and microwave on HIGH for 5 min. Stir.
3 Meanwhile, mix the remaining ingredients, binding them well together.
4 Form the mixture into 12 meatballs and arrange these on the cabbage bed, around the outside of the dish.
5 Cover and cook on HIGH for about 10 min or until cooked. Turn the dish during cooking if the oven does not have a turntable.
6 Stand for 5 min before serving.

450g (1lb) shredded cabbage
150ml (5fl oz) boiling beef stock
450g (1lb) lean minced beef
½ × 5ml tsp (½tsp) onion powder
1 × 5ml tsp (1tsp) mixed herbs
salt and pepper
1 egg, beaten

Sweet and sour meatballs (*serves 4–6*)

CALORIES: 1,140

1 Shape the minced beef into 2.5cm (1in) balls.
2 Place onion, salt, soup and lemon juice in a round dish or casserole.
3 Cover and microwave on HIGH for about 4–6 min or until boiling. Stir during cooking.
4 Stir mixture, add meatballs.
5 Cover and cook on HIGH for about 5–6 min or until cooked. Stir twice during the cooking period.
6 Add pineapple chunks and microwave on HIGH for a further 1½–2 min or until heated through.

450g (1lb) lean minced beef
1 large onion, peeled and finely chopped
½ × 5ml tsp (½tsp) salt
1 × 283g (10oz) can low-calorie tomato soup
3 × 15ml tbsp (3tbsp) lemon juice
1 × 454g (16oz) can pineapple chunks in natural juice, drained

Braised kidneys with orange (*serves 2*)

CALORIES: 437

1 Using scissors, make a small slit in the top of the frozen packs.
2 Place on a plate or in a shallow dish and microwave on HIGH for about 7–8 min, shaking the packs gently after 3 min. Leave to stand for 2 min.
3 Meanwhile, grate the orange rind before skinning the fruit and cutting into segments.
4 Turn the cooked kidneys into a suitable serving dish, stir in the orange segments and sprinkle the grated rind on top.
5 Cover and microwave on HIGH for about 1–2 min to reheat.
6 Serve garnished with chopped chives.

2 × 142g (5oz) individual packs braised kidneys in gravy, frozen
1 orange
chopped chives

4 minute steaks, each weighing
100g (4oz)
1 small onion, peeled and thinly
sliced
1 × 283g (10oz) can tomato
sauce
garlic salt to taste
chopped parsley

Minute steaks with onion and tomato sauce (serves 4)
CALORIES: 880

1 Pre-heat a microwave browning dish according to manufacturer's instructions.
2 Place the steaks on the base of the pre-heated dish, with the onion around the edges.
3 Microwave on HIGH for 2 min.
4 Turn steaks over and continue cooking on HIGH for a further 2–3 min or until steaks are cooked as preferred.
5 Arrange steaks in a serving dish and keep warm.
6 Mix together the drained onion, tomato sauce and garlic salt in a jug or bowl.
7 Cover and microwave on HIGH for 2–3 min or until bubbling.
8 Pour over steaks, garnish with parsley and serve.

leg of lamb weighing about
2kg (4lb)
salt
microwave unseasoned
browning mix

Roast leg of lamb (serves 4–6) colour opposite
CALORIES: 2,500

1 Rub salt into the skin and sprinkle the joint with the microwave unseasoned browning mix.
2 Shield the narrow end by wrapping in a small piece of aluminium foil to cover about 5cm (2in) of the meat. Foil must not touch the oven interior.
3 Place the joint on a microwave roasting rack or upturned saucer in a dish to catch the juices.
4 Microwave on HIGH for 18–20 min.
5 Pour off excess meat juices, remove the foil, turn joint over and microwave on HIGH for a further 18–20 min or until a thermometer inserted in the thickest part of the joint, avoiding the bone, reads 82°C (180°F) and juices run clear.
6 Cover joint with a tent of aluminium foil, shiny-side in, and leave to stand for about 10 min before serving.

1 × 2kg (4½lb) chicken at
room temperature, giblets
removed
microwave seasoning for
chicken (optional)

Chicken in-the-bag (serves 6)
CALORIES: 1,800

1 Truss the chicken so that the wings and legs are held firmly and close to the body to give a compact shape. Small pieces of foil may be used to shield wing tips and bone ends of legs.
2 Place the chicken, sprinkled with the seasoning, if used, in a roasting bag.
3 Slit or pierce the bag in 3–4 places, and tie the end loosely with string or an elastic band.
4 Place breast-side down on a microwave roasting rack or upturned saucer in a dish to catch the juices.
5 Cook on HIGH for 16 min.
6 Drain off excess juices, remove any pieces of foil and turn chicken over, breast-side up.
7 Cook on HIGH for a further 16 min or until a meat thermometer inserted in the thickest part of each thigh reads 85°C (185°F).
8 Cover with a tent of foil, shiny-side in, and leave to stand for 10–15 min, when the internal temperature should register 90°C (195°F), juices should run clear and the joints be flexible.
9 Remove the chicken from bag, garnish as preferred, carve and serve.

Roast Leg of Lamb (above);
Smothered Lamb Chops (page 67)

100g (4oz) sliced mushrooms
2 × 15ml tbsp (2tbsp) chopped
  red pepper
2 × 15ml tbsp (2tbsp) chopped
  green pepper
1 × 15ml tbsp (1tbsp) water
15g (½oz) cornflour
150ml (5fl oz) skimmed milk
275ml (½pt) chicken stock
salt and pepper
nutmeg
350g (12oz) cooked chicken,
  roughly chopped
1 × 15ml tbsp (1tbsp) low-fat
  natural yoghurt (optional)
sliced tomato
chopped parsley

Chicken à la king *(serves 4)* *colour page 19*
CALORIES: 650

1 Place mushrooms, chopped peppers and water in a suitable dish.
2 Cover and microwave on HIGH for about 2 min or until soft.
3 Blend the cornflour to a smooth paste with a little of the milk. Stir in the rest of the milk and the stock and add to the vegetables, mixing well together.
4 Cover and cook on HIGH for about 4–4½ min or until sauce has thickened. Stir during cooking.
5 Add salt, pepper and nutmeg to taste and stir in the chicken, mixing well.
6 Cover and microwave on HIGH for about 3 min or until heated through. Stir during cooking.
7 Stir in yoghurt, if used, and garnish with sliced tomato and chopped parsley.
8 Serve with cooked cabbage or heated bean sprouts in preference to boiled rice.

8 chicken drumsticks
50g (2oz) low-fat spread,
  melted
2 × 15ml tbsp (2tbsp) dried
  parsley flakes or chopped
  parsley
2 × 5ml tsp (2tsp) finely
  chopped chives
1 × 15ml tbsp (1tbsp) grated
  parmesan cheese (optional)
salt and pepper

Party drumsticks *(makes 8)*
CALORIES: 1,050

1 Remove skin and fat from drumsticks and brush sparingly with the melted low-fat spread.
2 Mix together the remaining ingredients and use to coat the drumsticks.
3 Place on a plate or in a shallow dish with the thicker parts towards the outside.
4 Microwave on HIGH for 6–7 min.
5 Turn drumsticks over and continue cooking on HIGH for a further 6–7 min or until fork tender.
6 Serve hot or cold.

4 × 175g (6oz) potatoes
175g (6oz) chopped onion
100g (4oz) chopped red pepper
2 × 15ml tbsp (2tbsp) water
25g (1oz) plain flour
275ml (½pt) turkey or chicken
  stock
1 × 15ml tbsp (1tbsp) tomato
  purée
1 × 15ml tbsp (1tbsp) french
  mustard
1 × 15ml tbsp (1tbsp)
  worcestershire sauce
225g (8oz) chopped cooked
  turkey
salt and pepper
chopped parsley

Boxing Day turkey *(serves 4)*
CALORIES: 1,000

1 Scrub the potatoes, prick, place in a circle on kitchen paper.
2 Microwave on HIGH for 12–14 min, turning the potatoes over after half the cooking time. Wrap in foil to keep warm.
3 Meanwhile, place onion, red pepper and water in a suitable bowl.
4 Cover and microwave on HIGH for 1½ min.
5 Stir in flour and microwave on HIGH for 1 min.
6 Add stock, tomato purée, mustard and worcestershire sauce, mixing well together.
7 Microwave on HIGH for 3 mins, stirring after every minute.
8 Stir in turkey, season to taste and microwave on HIGH for 2–2½ min, stirring after 1 min.
9 Unwrap potatoes, cut a lid from each and scoop out the centre, leaving a wall of potato inside the skin.
10 Sieve the potato and put into a piping bag fitted with a star nozzle.
11 Divide the turkey mixture among the potatoes and pipe the potato on top around the outside.
12 Brown under a pre-heated conventional grill and garnish with chopped parsley before serving with a salad.

Coated chicken portions (*serves 4*)

CALORIES: 1,200

1 Remove skin and fat from chicken portions.
2 Sprinkle the surface with the microwave seasoning.
3 Place in a single layer in a shallow dish approx 30 × 17.5cm (12 × 7in) with thicker pieces towards the outside.
4 Microwave on HIGH for 10–12 min.
5 Turn portions over and continue cooking on HIGH for a further 10–12 min or until tender.
6 Stand for 5 min before serving.

1 × 1½kg (3lb) roasting chicken, cut into 8 portions
microwave seasoning for chicken

Rabbit casserole (*serves 4*)

CALORIES: 552

1 Brown the rabbit joints in a non-stick fry-pan, sprayed with low-calorie vegetable oil, on a conventional cooker hob.
2 Meanwhile, place the onion, mushrooms and water in a suitable dish. Cover and microwave on HIGH for about 2 min or until soft.
3 Blend the cornflour with the milk, stir in the stock and add to the vegetables.
4 Cover and cook on HIGH for 3–3½ min or until sauce has thickened. Stir during cooking.
5 Season to taste, add the browned rabbit joints, coating them with the sauce.
6 Cover and cook on HIGH for 15–20 min or until rabbit is tender. Stir after 8 min and again after 15 min.
7 Serve garnished with watercress.

4 rabbit joints
1 medium onion, peeled and finely chopped
100g (4oz) sliced mushrooms
1 × 15ml tbsp (1tbsp) water
15g (½oz) cornflour
150ml (¼pt) skimmed milk
275ml (½pt) chicken stock
salt and pepper
watercress

450g (1lb) lean minced beef
1 medium onion, skinned and
  chopped
275ml (½pt) beef stock
225g (8oz) mushrooms sliced
salt and pepper

Minced beef with mushrooms *(serves 4)*
CALORIES: 772

1 Break down the mince well with a fork and mix with the chopped onion. Place in a large casserole.
2 Microwave on HIGH for 3 min.
3 Break down mince and stir mixture.
4 Microwave on HIGH for a further 3 min. Pour off excess fat and stir well.
5 Stir in stock, mushrooms and seasoning and mix well together.
6 Cover and microwave on HIGH for about 2–3 min or until mixture boils. Stir.
7 Reduce setting to LOW and cook for about 20 min or until meat and vegetables are cooked. Stir after 10 min.
8 Stir well and leave to stand, covered, for 5 min before serving.
9 If preferred, allow to cool, refrigerate and skim off any fat from the surface before reheating gently to serve.

VARIATIONS
1 *Minced beef stroganoff:* Proceed as above, but after cooking and before standing, stir in 125ml (5fl oz) natural low-fat yoghurt. If stroganoff is to be reheated, do not allow it to boil.
2 Follow the above recipe, cool, refrigerate and skim off any fat. Remove a slimmer's portion, turn the remaining mixture into a pie dish and top with cooked mashed potato. Reheat and serve as beef and mushroom pie for the rest of the family, browning the potato under a pre-heated conventional grill, if preferred.

450g (1lb) lean minced beef
1 medium onion, skinned and
  minced or grated
½ × 5ml tsp (½tsp) mixed
  herbs (optional)
1 × 5ml tsp (1tsp) chopped
  parsley
salt and pepper
worcestershire sauce

Minced beef patties *(serves 4–5)* *colour opposite*
CALORIES: 740

1 Mix together the minced beef, onion, herbs, if used, parsley and seasoning, and shape into 4–5 rounds about 1.25cm (½in) thick and 10cm (4in) in diameter.
2 Place either in a circle on kitchen paper on a plate or shallow round dish, or on a microwave roasting rack in a dish to catch juices.
3 Brush with worcestershire sauce and microwave on HIGH for 3 min. Pour off excess juices and reserve.
4 Turn patties over, brush with worcestershire sauce and microwave on HIGH for a further 3–4 min or until cooked as preferred. Pour off excess juices and reserve.
5 Leave patties to stand for 2–3 min before arranging on a heated serving plate.
6 Meanwhile, if liked, skim fat from reserved meat juices and reheat to serve separately with the cooked patties.

VARIATION
Browning dish meat patties
Prepare patties as above, but do not brush with worcestershire sauce. Place in microwave browning dish which has been pre-heated according to manufacturer's instructions. Microwave on HIGH for 3–4 min, turn over and cook for a further 3–4 min on HIGH or until cooked as preferred.

Minced Beef Patties in microwave browning dish (above); Roast Beef (page 66)

Vegetables

Vegetables are a healthy addition to any diet and are especially important to the slimmer. The majority of fresh vegetables in particular are not only low in calories but also contain essential vitamins and minerals and provide roughage. Vegetables should be thought of as a food rather than a 'filler'. There is growing interest today in non-meat main-course dishes made either from vegetables alone or vegetables combined with cheese or eggs. Good quality vegetables, correctly cooked, can be both satisfying and enjoyable.

A microwave oven cooks vegetables to perfection—crisp, almost chinese stir-fry style, but tender and full of colour and flavour. Also, since they are cooked in little or sometimes no water, there is maximum retention of vitamins and minerals. They can also be reheated satisfactorily and without deterioration, provided they were in prime condition before cooking and were correctly cooked.

Vegetables can also be blanched in small quantities, 450g (1lb) maximum, in a microwave oven, prior to freezing. To each 450g (1lb) vegetables allow approximately 75ml (3fl oz) water and blanch in a suitable covered dish for half the recommended cooking time, stirring at least twice during this period. After blanching, the vegetables should be drained immediately and plunged into ice-cold water, after which they should be drained, packed and frozen in the usual way.

HINTS ON COOKING VEGETABLES
1   Cook fresh vegetables in a covered serving dish. Small quantities of commercially frozen vegetables can be cooked in their pack which should be slit or pierced.
2   Add only 2–3 × 15ml tbsp (2–3tbsp) water when cooking most vegetables. The exceptions are jacket potatoes, corn-on-the-cob, mushrooms, spinach and courgettes which are cooked without water.
3   If you prefer softer vegetables, add more water to slow down the rate of cooking and allow the cooking time to be extended slightly.
4   Do not sprinkle salt directly on to vegetables since this can cause dehydration and overcooking. If it is desirable to add salt during cooking, dissolve it first in the cooking water before the vegetables are added. Correct seasoning after cooking if no salt has been added.
5   Pierce or prick the skins of whole vegetables such as jacket potatoes and tomatoes to prevent bursting during cooking.
6   Cut vegetables into even-sized pieces for even cooking results.
7   Do not overcook vegetables otherwise they will become tough. Remember, they will continue to cook during the standing time.
8   Arrange stalked or spear vegetables with the stalks towards the outside of the dish, and rearrange during cooking.
9   Quality, age and thickness of vegetables will affect the cooking time, so test for readiness during cooking.
10 Stir vegetables during cooking, and rotate dish if the oven does not have a turntable.
11 Always allow vegetables to stand before serving.
12 Reserve drained cooking liquid to add to soups and sauces.

Guide to cooking fresh vegetables

Vegetable	Quantity	Approx cooking time on HIGH setting	Special instructions	Approx standing time
asparagus spears	225g (8oz) 450g (1lb)	6–8 min 8–10 min	arrange stalks towards outside of dish; cooking time may vary, depending on thickness of spears	2 min 3 min

beans
  broad, shelled
  green, sliced
  green, whole
	450g (1lb)
	450g (1lb)
	450g (1lb)
		9–11 min
		8–10 min
		8–10 min
			stir during cooking
			stir during cooking
			rearrange during cooking
				2–3 min
				2–3 min
				2–3 min

beetroot, 2 whole	450g (1lb)	12–15 min	do not add water; wash and pierce skins; if either weighs more than 250g (8oz), cut in half	5 min
broccoli, spears	450g (1lb)	8–10 min	place stems towards outside of dish; rearrange during cooking	4 min
brussels sprouts	225g (8oz) 450g (1lb)	5–7 min 8–10 min	stir during cooking stir during cooking	2 min 2–3 min
cabbage, shredded	450g (1lb)	9–11 min	stir during cooking	2–3 min
carrots, sliced	225g (8oz) 450g (1lb)	7–8 min 10–12 min	stir during cooking stir during cooking	2 min 2–3 min

cauliflower
  florets
  whole
	450g (1lb)
	450g (1lb)
		9–11 min
		10–12 min
			stir during cooking
			rotate during cooking if oven does not have a turntable
				3–5 min
				5 min

celery, sliced	350g (12oz)	8–10 min	stir during cooking	2 min
corn-on-the-cob	2 × 225g (8oz)	6–8 min	do not add water; turn over after 3 min	2–3 min
courgettes, sliced	450g (1lb)	9–11 min	do not add water; stir gently during cooking	5 min
leeks, sliced	450g (1lb)	8–10 min	stir during cooking	2–3 min
mushrooms	225g (8oz)	3–5 min	do not add water	1–2 min
onions, sliced	225g (8oz)	4–6 min	stir during cooking	2 min
parsnips, sliced	450g (1lb)	8–10 min	stir during cooking	2 min
peas	450g (1lb)	6–8 min	stir during cooking	2 min

potatoes
  baked in their
  jackets
	1 × 175g (6oz)
	2 × 175g (6oz)
		4–5 min
		7–8 min
			place on kitchen paper; turn over after half the cooking time; stand, wrapped in foil shiny-side in	5 min
				5 min

Vegetable	Quantity	Approx cooking time on HIGH setting	Special instructions	Approx standing time
potatoes boiled	450g (1lb)	8–10 min	cut into even-sized pieces; stir during cooking	3 min
spinach	450g (1lb)	6–8 min	do not add water; turn dish during cooking if the oven does not have a turntable	2 min
swede/turnip, diced	450g (1lb)	10–15 min	stir during cooking; time will vary, depending on age	3 min
tomatoes, halved	225g (8oz)	3–4 min	do not add water; rearrange during cooking	2–3 min

Guide to cooking frozen vegetables

Vegetable	Quantity	Approx cooking time on HIGH setting	Special instructions	Approx standing time
asparagus	225g (8oz)	6–7 min	rearrange during cooking period	3 min
	450g (1lb)	9–12 min	rearrange during cooking period	5 min
beans				
broad	225g (8oz)	7–8 min	stir during cooking	3 min
green, whole	225g (8oz)	6–8 min	stir during cooking	3 min
or sliced	450g (1lb)	10–12 min	stir during cooking	5 min
broccoli spears	225g (8oz)	8–10 min	rearrange spears after 4 min	3–5 min
brussels sprouts	225g (8oz)	6–7 min	stir during cooking	3 min
	450g (1lb)	10–12 min	stir during cooking	3 min
cauliflower florets	225g (8oz)	7–8 min	stir during cooking	3 min
	450g (1lb)	10–12 min	stir during cooking	5 min
carrots				
sliced	225g (8oz)	7–8 min	stir during cooking	3 min
	450g (1lb)	10–12 min	stir during cooking	3 min
whole, baby	450g (1lb)	12–15 min	rearrange during cooking	3–5 min
corn-on-the-cob	1 ear	4–5 min	wrap in greaseproof paper; turn during cooking	2–3 min
	2 ears	6–7 min	wrap in greaseproof paper; turn during cooking	3 min

Vegetable Selection: Carrot Sticks, Whole Green Beans, Parsley Potatoes, Broccoli

Vegetable	Quantity	Approx cooking time on HIGH setting	Special instructions	Approx standing time
mixed vegetables	230g (8oz) pouch	5–6 min	cook in slit pouch; shake during cooking and standing time	2 min
peas	230g (8oz) pouch	5–6 min	cook in slit pouch; shake during cooking and standing time	2 min
	450g (1lb)	8–9 min	stir during cooking	2 min
spinach	225g (8oz)	6–8 min	do not add water; stir during cooking	2 min
	450g (1lb)	8–9 min	stir during cooking	2 min
swede/turnip, diced	450g (1lb)	10–12 min	stir during cooking	3 min
sweetcorn	225g (8oz)	4–6 min	stir during cooking	2 min

450g (1lb) finely shredded cabbage
2 medium eating apples, skinned, cored and chopped
salt and pepper
2 × 15ml tbsp (2tbsp) chicken stock

Cabbage and apple casserole (serves 4)
CALORIES: 144

1 Mix together all the ingredients and turn into a suitable casserole.
2 Cover and cook on HIGH for about 9–12 min or until tender. Stir during cooking period.
3 Stand, covered, for 2 min. Stir well before serving.

450g (1lb) carrots
2 × 15ml tbsp (2tbsp) water
salt and pepper
2 × 15ml tbsp (2tbsp) cranberry jelly

Cranberry glazed carrots (serves 4)
CALORIES: 186

1 Wash carrots. Small new baby carrots can be left whole, otherwise scrape and slice into rounds.
2 Place in casserole with the water.
3 Cover and cook on HIGH for 9–10 min or until just tender. Stir during cooking.
4 Add seasoning and toss the carrots in the jelly.
5 Reheat if necessary to melt jelly on HIGH for 1 minute.

225g (½lb) mushrooms, sliced if large
1 × 15ml tbsp (1tbsp) cornflour
275ml (½pt) skimmed milk
50g (2oz) grated cheese, preferably edam or austrian smoked
salt and pepper
dash of worcestershire sauce
low-calorie bread, toasted conventionally

Mushrooms in cheese sauce (serves 2)
CALORIES: 478

1 Place the mushrooms in a suitable dish with a very little stock or water.
2 Cover and microwave on HIGH for 2–3 min. Set aside.
3 Blend the cornflour with the milk in a jug and microwave on HIGH for about 3 min or until thick, stirring every minute.
4 Stir in the cheese, seasoning and worcestershire sauce together with the drained liquid from the cooked mushrooms.
5 Either pour the sauce over the mushrooms or fold the mushrooms into the sauce.
6 Serve on hot toasted bread as a main course.

Ratatouille *(serves 4–6)* *colour page 7*
CALORIES: 146

225g (8oz) sliced aubergines
1 clove garlic, crushed or finely chopped
225g (8oz) sliced onions
2 × 15ml tbsp (2tbsp) water
225g (8oz) sliced courgettes
1 red pepper, deseeded and thinly sliced
1 green pepper, deseeded and and thinly sliced
225g (8oz) skinned sliced tomatoes
pinch of rosemary
salt and pepper
chopped parsley

1 Sprinkle the sliced aubergines with salt and set aside for 30 min. Rinse thoroughly, drain and pat dry on kitchen paper.
2 Place the garlic, onions and water in a large dish, cover and microwave on HIGH for 2–3 min or until soft.
3 Stir in the aubergines, courgettes and peppers.
4 Cover and continue on HIGH for 5 min.
5 Stir in the tomatoes, rosemary and seasoning to taste.
6 Cover and cook on HIGH for 12–15 min or until all vegetables are tender. Stir during cooking period.
7 Serve hot with fish or meat dishes, or cold as a starter, sprinkled with chopped parsley.

Bavarian red cabbage *(serves 4)* *colour page 84*
CALORIES: 270

450g (1lb) red cabbage, finely shredded
1 medium onion, peeled and finely chopped
1 large eating apple, peeled, cored and chopped
1 × 5ml tsp (1tsp) brown sugar
½ × 5ml tsp (½tsp) ground cloves
pinch of cinnamon
salt and pepper
4 × 15ml tbsp (4tbsp) red wine vinegar
1 bayleaf

1 Mix all ingredients together and turn into a suitable casserole.
2 Cover and microwave on HIGH for 10 min.
3 Stir, recover and continue on HIGH for a further 10–15 min or until cooked.
4 Remove bay leaf and stir before serving.

Saucy aubergines *(serves 4–5)*
CALORIES: 205

675g (1½lb) aubergines, wiped
1 medium onion, peeled and finely chopped
salt
2 × 15ml tbsp (2tbsp) lemon juice
pinch of rosemary
3 tomatoes, cut into quarters
1 × 150ml (5fl oz) carton natural low-fat yoghurt
cress

1 Slice the aubergines rather thickly, remove seeds if necessary and cut into fairly large cubes.
2 Mix with the remaining ingredients, except the tomatoes and yoghurt.
3 Turn into a suitable dish.
4 Cover and microwave on HIGH for 9–10 min.
5 Stir, add tomatoes and yoghurt.
6 Cover and heat gently on LOW for about 6 min.
7 Stand for 2 min and sprinkle with cress before serving.

Caraway cabbage *(serves 4) colour opposite*
CALORIES: 129–161 *(depending on weight of cabbage)*

1 Place the shredded cabbage and water in a round casserole.
2 Cover and microwave on HIGH for 10–12 min. Stir during cooking. Drain.
3 Toss the cabbage lightly in the yoghurt and caraway seeds and season to taste before serving.

450–675g (1–1½lb) finely shredded cabbage
2 × 15ml tbsp (2tbsp) water
150ml (5fl oz) natural low-fat yoghurt
½ × 5ml tsp (½tsp) caraway seeds
salt and pepper

Green beans piquant *(serves 4)*
CALORIES: 92

1 Place beans with water in a round casserole.
2 Cover and microwave on HIGH for about 12 min or until tender. Stir during cooking. Drain.
3 Mix the mustard with the worcestershire sauce and stir into the beans.
4 Season and sprinkle lightly with grated parmesan cheese before serving.

450g (1lb) green beans, washed and cut into even-sized pieces
2 × 15ml tbsp (2tbsp) water
1 × 5ml tsp (1tsp) made mustard
2 × 5ml tsp (2tsp) worcestershire sauce
pepper
grated parmesan cheese

Stuffed rainbow peppers *(serves 4) colour page 11*
CALORIES: 735

1 Cut the peppers in half lengthways, remove seeds and membrane. Arrange in a single layer in a suitable dish.
2 Mix together the minced beef, onion and breadcrumbs and bind together with the beaten egg and 50ml (2fl oz) of the measured beef stock.
3 Stuff the peppers with the mixture.
4 Pour the remaining 150ml (6fl oz) stock into the dish with the peppers and cover the dish with clingfilm.
5 Microwave on HIGH for about 10–15 min or until peppers are cooked. Rearrange the peppers during cooking.
6 Drain the peppers, sprinkle with chopped yellow pepper and serve with a side-salad.

4 large green or red peppers
1 × 411g (15oz) can minced beef
1 small onion, skinned and minced or finely chopped
50g (2oz) low-calorie breadcrumbs
1 egg, beaten
200ml (8fl oz) beef stock
salt and pepper
3–4 × 15ml tbsp (3–4tbsp) chopped yellow pepper

Cauliflower polonaise *(serves 4)*
CALORIES: 431

1 Shell and finely chop the eggs.
2 Prepare the cauliflower, remove hard core from the base and place with the water in a suitable dish.
3 Cover and microwave on HIGH for 10–12 min or until tender crisp. Turn the dish during the cooking period if the oven does not have a turntable.
4 Drain, season and leave to stand, covered.
5 Meanwhile, melt the low-fat spread in a small bowl on HIGH for about 1 min.
6 Stir in the breadcrumbs and microwave on HIGH for about 2 min or until golden, stirring after 1 min.
7 Mix with the chopped eggs and parsley and sprinkle over the cooked cauliflower.

2 eggs, hard-boiled
1 cauliflower weighing about 600g (1¼lb)
4 × 15ml tbsp (4tbsp) water
salt and pepper
25g (1oz) low-fat spread
25g (1oz) low-calorie breadcrumbs
1–2 × 15ml tbsp (1–2tbsp) finely chopped parsley

Caraway Cabbage (above); Bavarian Red Cabbage (page 83)

4 × 175g (6oz) potatoes
100g (4oz) chopped ham
2 × 15ml tbsp (2tbsp) skimmed
   milk
salt and pepper
paprika or chopped parsley

Stuffed baked potatoes *(serves 4)*
CALORIES: 770

1 Wash and dry potatoes and prick thoroughly.
2 Place in a circle on absorbent kitchen paper in the oven.
3 Microwave on HIGH for 6 min.
4 Turn each potato over and continue cooking on HIGH for a further 6–8 min or until tender.
5 Either slit the top of each potato or cut in half lengthways.
6 Scoop out the soft potato and mix with the ham and milk, seasoning to taste.
7 Pile the mixture back into the skins and sprinkle with paprika or chopped parsley.
8 Reheat if necessary for about 2 min only.
9 Serve with salad as a light lunch or supper dish.

VARIATIONS
Substitute left-over cooked meat or fish, or crumbled cooked bacon for ham.
Omit ham and milk and add 100g (4oz) cottage cheese with chives or onion and peppers to the mashed potato.
Substitute 100g (4oz) cooked shrimps or prawns for ham.
Omit ham and milk and stir 100ml (4fl oz) natural low-fat yoghurt and 2 × 15ml tbsp (2tbsp) scissored chives into the mashed potato.

1 head of celery
1 × 5ml tsp (1tsp) salt
1 × 5ml tsp (1tsp) basil
1 mixed herbs stock cube
425ml (¾pt) water

Celery braised with herbs *(serves 4)*
CALORIES: 40

1 Prepare the celery and cut into 5–7.5cm (2–3in) lengths. Place in a fairly shallow dish.
2 Mix together the remaining ingredients and pour over the celery.
3 Cover and microwave on HIGH for about 14–15 min or until celery is tender. Stir during cooking.
4 Stand, covered, for 2–3 min before serving, reserving any excess juices for future use in soups, sauces or dishes requiring stock.

VARIATIONS
Celery au gratin
Cook celery as above, drain off excess juices, sprinkle top with low-calorie breadcrumbs and brown under a pre-heated conventional grill.

Celery cheese
Cook celery as above, drain off excess juices and sprinkle top with grated cheese. Either return dish, uncovered, to the oven for 1–2 min to melt cheese, or melt and brown it under a pre-heated conventional grill.

1 medium cabbage, finely
   shredded
50ml (2fl oz) water
75g (3oz) philadelphia cheese,
   softened at room
   temperature
1 × 5ml tsp (1tsp) dill seeds
salt and freshly ground black
   pepper

Dressed cabbage *(serves 4)*
CALORIES: 366

1 Place the shredded cabbage and water in a suitable casserole.
2 Cover and microwave on HIGH for about 9–12 min or until tender. Stir or shake after 4 min.
3 Stir in the cheese, dill seeds and seasoning.
4 Cover and microwave on HIGH for about 1 min until heated through.
5 Stand, covered, for 2 min before serving.

Stuffed marrow slices *(serves 4)*
CALORIES: 604

1 vegetable marrow, weighing
  about 1kg (2¼lb)
225g (8oz) lean minced beef
1 medium onion, peeled and
  chopped
50g (2oz) mushrooms, chopped
1 × 397g (14oz) can peeled
  tomatoes in tomato juice
salt and pepper

1 Cut the marrow into 4cm (1½in) thick slices and remove seeds.
2 Arrange the slices in a single layer in a suitable dish, placing any smaller slices in the centre of the dish.
3 Cover and cook on HIGH for 6 min, turning the dish after 3 min if the oven does not have a turntable. Drain off surplus liquid.
4 To make stuffing, place the minced beef and onion in a dish, cover and cook on HIGH for about 5 min, stirring and breaking up the minced beef during cooking. Drain off fat.
5 Turn the tomatoes and their juice into a bowl and roughly chop the tomatoes.
6 Add the mushrooms and seasoning to the minced beef and moisten with 2 × 15ml tbsp (2tbsp) of the tomato mixture.
7 Fill the marrow slices with this mixture.
8 Cover and cook on HIGH for about 7–8 min or until tender. Rotate the dish during cooking if the oven does not have a turntable.
9 Leave to stand, covered, while heating the remaining tomato mixture on HIGH for about 2–3 min or until hot.
10 Either pour the tomato mixture over the marrow slices or serve separately.

Italian-style courgettes *(serves 4)*
CALORIES: 279

450g (1lb) small courgettes,
  thinly sliced
3 sticks of celery, thinly sliced
200ml (8fl oz) tomato juice
salt and pepper
pinch of thyme
pinch of basil
dash of garlic salt

1 Mix the courgettes and celery together in a suitable casserole.
2 Combine the remaining ingredients and pour over the vegetables.
3 Cover and microwave on HIGH for about 10–12 min or until vegetables are cooked. Stir during cooking.

Tomatoes on toast *(serves 2–3) colour page 29*
CALORIES: 106–141 *(depending on bread slices used)*

1 × 397g (14oz) can peeled
  tomatoes in tomato juice
2–3 slices low-calorie bread,
  toasted conventionally

1 Turn the contents of the can into a 500ml (1pt) round casserole.
2 Cover and microwave on HIGH for 1½–2 min or until tomatoes are heated but still whole.
3 Stand for 2 min before serving on the hot toasted bread.

Stuffed courgettes *(serves 3)*
CALORIES: 846

1 Place minced beef in a suitable dish.
2 Cover and cook on HIGH for 2–3 min or until no longer pink. Stir after 1½ min. Drain off fat.
3 Arrange the halved courgettes in a single layer in a fairly shallow flameproof dish. Cover and cook on HIGH for 7 min.
4 Scoop out most of the flesh, leaving a 0.5cm (¼in) thick shell.
5 Chop the flesh and add to the minced beef. Season.
6 Stuff the courgette shells with the mixture.
7 Cover and cook on HIGH for 10 min or until cooked. Turn dish after 5 min if oven does not have a turntable.
8 Sprinkle tops with grated cheese.
9 Brown under a pre-heated conventional grill before serving.

350g (12oz) lean minced beef
450g (1lb) courgettes, washed, end trimmed and cut in half lengthwise
salt and pepper
40g (1½oz) grated cheese, preferably edam

Main course vegetable medley au gratin *(serves 3–4)*
colour opposite
CALORIES: 834

1 Arrange cauliflower florets in a suitable dish with stems towards the outside of the dish. Add 2 × 15ml tbsp (2tbsp) water.
2 Cover and microwave on HIGH for 10 min, turning the dish during cooking if the oven does not have a turntable.
3 Turn the cauliflower into a colander to drain.
4 Place the carrots and onions in the same cooking dish with 2 × 15ml tbsp (2tbsp) water, cover and microwave on HIGH for about 8 min, shaking the dish or stirring the vegetables after 8 min.
5 Drain and mix with the cauliflower. Season.
6 Place the mixed vegetables in a suitable round deep soufflé dish or casserole. Pour over the tomato juice. Stir.
7 Mix most of the cheese with the breadcrumbs and sprinkle on top. Cover top surface with remaining cheese.
8 Microwave on HIGH for about 5 min to reheat.
9 Place under a pre-heated conventional grill for a crisply browned topping.
10 Garnish with the chopped hard-boiled eggs and parsley.

450g (1lb) frozen cauliflower florets
225g (8oz) fresh carrots, scraped and sliced into rings
2 medium onions, sliced
salt and pepper
150ml (¼pt) tomato juice
100g (4oz) grated edam or austrian smoked cheese
50g (2oz) low-calorie brown breadcrumbs
2 hard-boiled eggs, finely chopped
chopped parsley

Baked jacket potatoes *(serves 1) colour page 45*
CALORIES: 150

1 Wash and dry the potatoes. Prick the skins with a fork.
2 Arrange in a circle on kitchen paper in the oven.
3 Microwave on HIGH for about 12–14 min, turning the potatoes over after half the cooking time.
4 Leave to stand, wrapped in foil, shiny-side inwards, for 5 min before serving.

1 × 175g (6oz) potatoes

VARIATIONS
1 × 175g (6oz) potato will require about 4–5 min on HIGH plus standing time.
2 × 175g (6oz) potatoes will require about 7–9 min on HIGH plus standing time.

Note Cooked jacket potatoes will keep warm for up to 30 min in foil.

Main Course Vegetable Medley au Gratin (above)

89

Desserts

Relinquishing or rejecting calorie-laden desserts is probably one of the most difficult decisions for many people to make, although we can all live quite healthily without them. Fortunately, however, there are many desserts which the slimmer can still enjoy without that feeling of guilt. The use of fruit, skimmed milk, gelatine, yoghurt, cornflour in permitted amounts, calorie-free sweeteners and flavourings can make tempting desserts which taste as good as they look.

Fresh fruit is now available throughout the year, and if you own a freezer you can freeze soft fruits when they are in season, ready to make delicious desserts at any time. Alternatively, you can buy commercially frozen fruit, or use fruit canned in natural unsweetened juice or water, so there is no excuse for eating calorie-laden, time-consuming, stodgy puddings or rich pastry-based desserts, even when entertaining. Baked apples which can take up to an hour to cook conventionally are ready in minutes in a microwave oven.

The recipes in this section will, I hope, convince you that a satisfying end to an enjoyable low-calorie meal is possible, and more especially with a microwave oven to help you.

HINTS ON COOKING DESSERTS
1 Desserts which require to be cooled or refrigerated before serving should be cooked well in advance of mealtimes, while those which are to be served hot can be made beforehand and quickly reheated in the microwave oven when required, perhaps even while you are eating the main course.
2 Fruit cooked in a microwave oven normally requires less sweetening and retains its natural colour, shape, texture and fresh flavour.
3 Always cook fruit which is to be stewed or poached in a covered container, and cut it into even-sized pieces if it is not to be left whole.
4 Pierce or prick shiny-skinned whole fruit such as apples before cooking to prevent bursting.
5 Dried fruit, which is much higher in calories than fresh fruit, can be cooked very quickly by microwave energy and without overnight soaking.
6 To make whole fruit easier to skin, place it in the microwave oven for a few seconds. It will be much juicier, too.
7 Desserts based on egg custard require attention to prevent overcooking or curdling and should preferably be cooked more slowly on LOW setting.
8 Fruit cooked straight from the freezer should be gently stirred during cooking and the dish should be rotated if the oven does not have a turntable.
9 When defrosting fruit which is not to be cooked, avoid over-thawing it in the oven. Remove it from the oven while it is still slightly icy and leave it to defrost completely during standing time. Stir or shake the dish gently during defrosting.
10 Use your microwave oven to dissolve quickly gelatine and commercial jellies (see Slimmer's short cuts, page 24).
11 Make desserts appealing to the eye. Cook and serve in individual dishes where possible, and top with a sprinkling of spice, finely grated lemon or orange rind, twists made from thinly cut fruit slices, or a few whole berries, especially if the dessert is fruit based.
12 Try to adapt some of your own favourite low-calorie desserts, using the hints and similar recipes in this book as guidelines.

Cooking fresh fruit

Fruit	Quantity	Approx cooking time on HIGH setting	Approx standing time
apples			
stewed	450g (1lb)	6–8 min	1–2 min
baked	1 medium	2–3 min	2–3 min
	2 medium	3–5 min	3 min
	4 medium	5–8 min	3–4 min
apricots, stewed	450g (1lb)	6–8 min	1–2 min
bilberries, blackberries, cranberries, loganberries	450g (1lb)	3–4 min	2 min
blackcurrants, redcurrants	450g (1lb)	3–4 min	1–2 min
cherries, stoned/pitted	450g (1lb)	4–6 min	1–2 min
gooseberries	450g (1lb)	3–4 min	2 min
peaches, skinned, stoned and halved	3 good sized	4–5 min	2 min
pears, skinned, cored and halved	4 medium	5–6 min	1–2 min
plums, damsons, stoned	450g (1lb)	3–4 min	2 min
rhubarb, cut into 2.5cm (1in) lengths	450g (1lb)	6–8 min	2–3 min

Raspberry wine jellies *(serves 4) colour page 41*
CALORIES: 520

1 raspberry flavoured jelly
275ml (½pt) water
275ml (½pt) dry red wine
low-calorie dessert topping, commercial or home-made
few fresh or frozen raspberries

1 Place cut up jelly cubes and water in a Pyrex measuring jug.
2 Microwave on HIGH for about 1½–2 min or until jelly has melted. Stir after 1 min.
3 Stir in wine, mixing well together.
4 Pour into 4 individual dishes, cool and refrigerate until set. Defrost frozen raspberries if necessary.
5 Top with low-calorie dessert topping and a few raspberries.

Low-calorie dessert topping
CALORIES: 36

50g (2oz) low-fat dry skimmed milk powder
2 × 5ml tsp (2tsp) lemon juice
few drops of calorie-free liquid sweetener
few drops of vanilla essence

1 Make up the milk powder to 150ml (¼pt) with iced water and stir in the lemon juice, sweetener and vanilla.
2 Whisk by hand or with an electric food mixer until very frothy, doubled in volume and thick enough to hold the trail of the whisk.
3 Can be made up to 30 min before it is required and preferably chilled in the refrigerator.

91

Cooking dried fruit in a microwave oven

1 Place dried prunes, apricots, figs, etc in a suitable dish or casserole.
2 Using 1½ times the amount of liquid to fruit, pour over sufficient water, cold tea, wine or wine and water mixed to cover.
3 Cover tightly and cook on HIGH for about 5 min.
4 Stir, re-cover and cook on HIGH for a further 5 min.
5 Leave to stand, covered, for at least 30 min to rehydrate.
6 Cool, refrigerate and serve.

Blackberry and Brandy Mousse (page 117); Strawberry Yoghurt Whip (page 117)

Bananas in spiced orange sauce *(serves 4–6) colour page 95*
CALORIES: 410

1 Peel bananas, cut in half lengthwise and then cut each half in two crosswise. Sprinkle with lemon juice.
2 Blend cornflour with orange juice in a suitable jug and stir in cinnamon and nutmeg.
3 Microwave sauce on HIGH for about 2 min or until thickened. Stir during cooking and at the end of the cooking period.
4 Arrange the cut bananas in a single layer in the base of a shallow dish and pour the sauce over them, turning to coat with the sauce.
5 Sprinkle the grated orange rind on top.
6 Microwave on HIGH for about 3 min or until bananas are hot, but still holding their shape. Turn the dish during the cooking period if the oven does not have a turntable.
7 Leave to stand for a few minutes before serving.

4 medium bananas
lemon juice
150ml (5fl oz) natural unsweetened orange juice
1 level 5ml tsp (1 level tsp) cornflour
½ level 5ml tsp (½ level tsp) cinnamon
½ level 5ml tsp (½ level tsp) nutmeg
finely grated rind of 1 orange

Fluffy meringues *(makes about 30)*
CALORIES: 679

1 Using a fork to mix, add enough sieved icing sugar to the egg white to give a stiff mixture which can be rolled between the palms of the hand.
2 Roll into small balls the size of a large marble (4 balls should weigh about 25g (1oz)).
3 Arrange the balls, 4 at a time and well apart, on kitchen paper on a cool (ie room temperature) round flat Pyrex plate.
4 Microwave on HIGH for 1–1½ min. During this time there will be a dramatic increase in size as the balls puff up.
5 Repeat with remaining mixture, using a cool plate each time. The plate must *not* be hot. *Do not overcook* —timing is critical.
6 Sandwich together with low-calorie dessert topping or serve with ice cream.

VARIATION
Sprinkle instant coffee powder on to the mixture before cooking.

half an egg white
approx 175g (6oz) sieved icing sugar

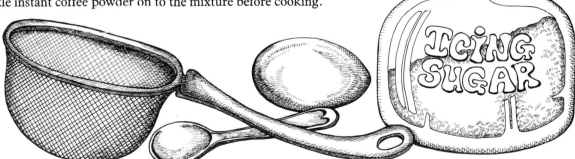

2 cans One Cal bitter orange
drink
1 sachet powdered gelatine
4 × 15ml tbsp (4tbsp) water
2 fresh oranges, skinned and
segmented

Bitter orange jelly (serves 4)
CALORIES: 162

1 Empty the bitter orange drink into a mixing bowl or jug.
2 Sprinkle the gelatine over the water in a small bowl and leave to soak for a few minutes.
3 Microwave on HIGH for 20–30 sec or until the gelatine has dissolved. Do not allow to boil. Stir and leave to cool a little before stirring into the bitter orange.
4 Add orange segments, pour into serving dish and refrigerate until set.

450g (1lb) fresh rhubarb, cut
into 2.5cm (1in) lengths
boiling water
rind and juice of 1 orange
1 medium banana
calorie-free liquid sweetener
(optional)
red food colouring (optional)
2 egg whites
25g (1oz) caster sugar

Rhubarb and banana swirl (serves 4–6) colour opposite
CALORIES: 383

1 Place the rhubarb in a suitable dish and cover with boiling water. Leave to stand for 5 min to reduce acidity. Drain well and pat dry on absorbent kitchen paper.
2 Return rhubarb to the dish, add the orange juice, cover and microwave on HIGH for 5 min or until tender. Stir during cooking. Leave to cool.
3 Peel and chop the banana and put into a blender with the cooked rhubarb to purée.
4 Add liquid sweetener and food colouring, if used.
5 Whisk the egg whites until stiff, add the sugar and whisk again until stiff.
6 Swirl the egg whites through the purée without folding in completely.
7 Turn mixture into 4–6 individual dishes and refrigerate.
8 Sprinkle tops with the orange rind before serving.

425ml (¾pt) skimmed milk
3 eggs, beaten
25g (1oz) caster sugar or
equivalent calorie-free
sweetener
grated nutmeg (optional)

Baked egg custard (serves 3)
CALORIES: 390–502 (depending whether sugar is used)

1 Heat milk in a suitable jug on HIGH for about 1½min or until warm.
2 Pour over the beaten eggs and sugar or sweetener. Stir well to mix.
3 Pour through a sieve into a 750ml (1½pt) round dish.
4 Sprinkle with grated nutmeg, if used.
5 Cover this dish with clingfilm and place it in a larger round dish, approx 1½ litre (3pt) capacity, containing 300ml (12fl oz) boiling water.
6 Microwave on LOW for about 15–20 min or until centre of custard is wobbly but not runny. Rotate dish gently during cooking if the oven does not have a turntable.
7 Remove the custard dish from the water bath and uncover.
8 Leave to cool and refrigerate before serving. The centre will set as the custard cools.

VARIATIONS
Individual custards
Divide the mixture among 4 individual serving dishes and arrange in a circle in the oven. Microwave on LOW for about 10–12 min or until just set. Rearrange during cooking if the oven does not have a turntable, and remove individually if some cook faster than others.

Individual crème brûlée (for non-slimmers)
Follow instructions for individual custards, cool and refrigerate. Just before serving, cover top surface thickly with demerara sugar and quickly flash under a pre-heated conventional grill to caramelise.

Bananas in Spiced Orange Sauce (page 93); Rhubarb and Banana Swirl (above)

450g (1lb) cooking apples,
   peeled, cored and sliced
25g (1oz) dates, chopped finely
calorie-free sweetener
   (optional)
2 egg whites
good pinch of cornflour
good pinch of cream of tartar
25g (1oz) caster sugar or
   equivalent sugar substitute

Apple and date meringue *(serves 3–4)*
CALORIES: 260–372 *(depending whether sugar is used)*

1 Place the prepared apples and dates in a 750ml (1½pt) flameproof dish, mixing them well together.
2 Cover and microwave on HIGH for about 6–8 min or until apples are cooked. Stir well to mix. Add artificial sweetener if found necessary.
3 Beat the egg whites with the cornflour and cream of tartar until stiff. Add the sugar or sugar substitute and beat again until stiff.
4 Spread the meringue over the fruit, sealing to the edge of the dish. Roughen up the surface into peaks or swirls with a knife.
5 Microwave on LOW for about 6–8 min or until the meringue has set.
6 Brown the top for a few minutes under a pre-heated conventional grill.
7 Serve immediately.

VARIATION
Substitute rhubarb for apples.

450g (1lb) fresh raspberries
8–12 white marshmallows

Raspberry mallow delights *(serves 4)*
CALORIES: 292

1 Reserve 4 raspberries and place the remainder in a suitable dish.
2 Cover and microwave on HIGH for 3–3½ min.
3 Spoon the raspberries into 4 suitable individual dishes and top each dish with 2–3 marshmallows.
4 Arrange the dishes in a circle in the oven and microwave on HIGH for about 45–60 sec or until the marshmallows have melted. Watch carefully and do not overheat.
5 Stand for 2–3 min before serving hot, topped with the reserved raspberries. If serving cold, refrigerate and top with the reserved raspberries immediately before serving.

VARIATIONS
Substitute blackberries, blackcurrants or strawberries for raspberries. Use a mixture of pink and white marshmallows.

4 medium eating apples
4 × 15ml tbsp (4tbsp) water

Baked apples *(serves 4) colour page 23*
CALORIES: 160

1 Core the apples and prick the skins with the tines of a fork.
2 Arrange in a circle in a suitable shallow round dish and add the water.
3 Cover with clingfilm and microwave on HIGH for about 5–6 min, depending on the type of apple.
4 Stand for 2–3 min. Spoon the juice over the apples before serving.
To cook 1 medium apple, use 1 × 15ml tbsp (1tbsp) water on HIGH for about 2½–3min.
To cook 2 medium apples, use 2 × 15ml tbsp (2tbsp) water on HIGH for about 3–3½ min.

VARIATION
Baked stuffed apples
Use cooking apples and fill the centre of each with dried fruit, dates or, for those who are not weight-conscious, with mincemeat. Mix calorie-free sweetener with the water, if preferred.

Fresh orange whip *(serves 4)* *colour page 41*
CALORIES: 432

4 medium oranges
1 × 15g (½oz) sachet powdered
  gelatine
2 eggs

1 Grate finely the rind of 2 oranges. Cut 4–5 thin slices from one of the remaining 2 oranges and reserve for decoration.
2 Squeeze the juice from the 3 oranges and the remainder of the fourth orange. Stir in the grated rind.
3 Make the juice and rind up to 425ml (¾pt) with water.
4 Place 2 × 15ml tbsp (2tbsp) of the juice in a suitable small bowl. Sprinkle in the gelatine and leave to soak for a few minutes.
5 Meanwhile, separate the eggs and beat the yolks until light and creamy. Stir in the orange juice.
6 Place the gelatine and water in the microwave on HIGH for 15–30 sec. Stir until gelatine has dissolved. Do not allow to boil.
7 Stir the dissolved gelatine into the orange juice mixture.
8 Whip the egg whites until stiff and fold lightly into the mixture.
9 Turn into a serving bowl and refrigerate until set.
10 Cut one of the reserved orange slices to the centre and twist; cut the remaining slices in half.
11 Arrange the halved orange slices around the outside of the set mixture and place the twisted slice in the centre before serving.

Lemon mousse *(serves 6–8)*
CALORIES: 592

4 eggs, separated
3 × 15ml tbsp (3tbsp) lemon
  juice
5 × 15ml tbsp (5tbsp) water
1 × 15g (½oz) sachet powdered
  gelatine
grated rind of 1 lemon
50g (2oz) caster sugar or
  equivalent sugar substitute
lemon twists

1 Place the lightly beaten egg yolks, lemon juice, water and gelatine in a suitable bowl and mix well together.
2 Microwave on HIGH for about 1 min or until gelatine has dissolved. Do not allow mixture to boil; stir after each 30 sec.
3 Stir in the grated rind and leave mixture to cool.
4 Whisk the egg whites until stiff. Add the sugar or sugar substitute and whisk again until stiff.
5 Fold the beaten egg whites into the lemon mixture and turn into a glass serving dish or individual dishes.
6 Refrigerate until set.
7 Decorate with lemon twists before serving.

VARIATION
Orange mousse
Use orange juice and rind instead of lemon. Proceed as above and decorate with orange twists or segments.

Blancmange
CALORIES: 560

1 sachet flavoured blancmange
550ml (1pt) skimmed milk
calorie-free sweetener to taste
fresh fruit (optional)

1 Blend the blancmange powder with a little of the measured milk in a suitable jug and gradually stir in the rest of the milk.
2 Microwave on HIGH for about 5 min or until thick, stirring after every 2 min.
3 Add sweetener to taste. Stir well.
4 Pour into a rinsed mould or serving dish, or individual dishes and leave to cool.
5 Refrigerate until set.
6 Unmould and/or decorate with fresh fruit as preferred before serving.

450g (1lb) cooking apples,
  peeled, cored and sliced
25g (1oz) dates, chopped finely
  or minced
1 × 15ml tbsp (1tbsp) water
2 × 5ml tsp (2tsp) lemon juice
2 egg whites
chopped nuts (optional)

Apple snow (*serves 4*) *colour opposite*
CALORIES: 260

1 Place the apples, dates, water and lemon juice in a suitable dish.
2 Cover and microwave on HIGH for about 6–8 min or until fruit is very soft.
3 Beat well, sieve or liquidise to give a thick purée.
4 Leave to cool.
5 Whip the egg whites to a stiff foam and fold them into the cooled purée.
6 Turn the mixture into individual serving dishes and refrigerate until well chilled.
7 Sprinkle with a few chopped nuts, if liked, before serving.

VARIATIONS
Substitute pears for apples and proceed as above, but cook the fruit on HIGH for about 8–10 min, or until very soft.
Use damsons, gooseberries or blackcurrants instead of apples. Omit dates and add calorie-free sweetener to taste to the fruit after cooking it on HIGH for about 3–6 min or until very soft.

350g (12oz) strawberries, fresh
  or defrosted if frozen
juice of 1 orange
1 × 15g (½oz) sachet powdered
  gelatine
2 × 15ml tbsp (2tbsp) water
1 × 142g (5oz) carton low-fat
  yoghurt, natural or
  strawberry flavoured
calorie-free sweetener
  (optional)
2 egg whites
sliced or small whole
  strawberries to decorate

Individual strawberry soufflés (*serves 6*)
CALORIES: 227

1 Combine the strawberries and orange juice and liquidise or sieve to make a purée.
2 Sprinkle the gelatine into the water in a small bowl and leave to soak for a few minutes.
3 Microwave on HIGH for about 20–30 sec to dissolve the gelatine. Stir, watch carefully and do not allow to boil.
4 Stir the dissolved gelatine and leave to cool slightly before stirring it into the purée.
5 Fold in the yoghurt and sweetener, if used. The mixture should now be cold.
6 Whisk the egg whites to a stiff foam and fold into the cold mixture.
7 Spoon into individual dishes and chill in the refrigerator.
8 Decorate with sliced or whole strawberries before serving.

1 fresh orange
175ml (6fl oz) natural
  unsweetened orange juice
275ml (½pt) natural low-fat
  yoghurt
1 × 15g (½oz) sachet powdered
  gelatine
4 × 15ml tbsp (4tbsp) water
2 egg whites
sprigs of fresh mint (optional)

Orange sorbet (*serves 4*)
CALORIES: 265

1 Grate the orange rind and add to the orange juice.
2 Stir in the yoghurt, mixing well.
3 Sprinkle the gelatine into the water in a suitable cup or small bowl and leave to soak for a few minutes.
4 Microwave on HIGH for about 30 sec to dissolve the gelatine. Do not allow to boil. Stir well.
5 Add the dissolved gelatine to the orange and yoghurt mixture, stirring well to mix thoroughly.
6 Leave mixture until just beginning to thicken and set.
7 Fold in the beaten egg whites, pour the mixture into a suitable container and freeze for several hours.
8 Remove the pith from the orange and cut into segments.
9 Scoop or spoon the sorbet into tall glasses with alternate layers of orange segments.
10 Garnish, if liked, with sprigs of fresh mint.

Compôte of Dried Fruit (page 100); Apple Snow (above)

225g (8oz) mixed dried fruit salad, ie prunes, apricots, apples, peaches
550ml (1pt) boiling water
juice of 1 orange
strip of orange peel

Compôte of dried fruit *(serves 4)* *colour page 99*
CALORIES: 400

1 Place all the ingredients in a suitably large casserole.
2 Cover tightly and microwave on HIGH for 5 min.
3 Stir and microwave on HIGH for a further 5 min.
4 Leave to stand, covered, for at least 30 min to rehydrate.
5 Cool and refrigerate.
6 Remove orange peel before serving.

4 medium peaches, skinned, halved and stoned
cinnamon
1 × 142g (5oz) carton low-fat yoghurt, natural, peach and redcurrant, or peach melba
nutmeg (optional)

Spiced peaches with yoghurt *(serves 4–8)*
CALORIES: 211

1 Arrange peach halves around the outside of a large round plate and sprinkle with cinnamon.
2 Microwave on HIGH for 3–6 min, depending on size, turning the plate during cooking if the oven does not have a turntable.
3 Cool and refrigerate until well chilled.
4 Serve topped with yoghurt and sprinkled with nutmeg, if used.

150ml (5fl oz) water
1 × 15ml tbsp (1tbsp) lemon juice
few strips of lemon rind
calorie-free liquid sweetener (optional)
4 firm pears
toasted flaked almonds

Spiked pears *(serves 4)*
CALORIES: 264

1 Place the water, lemon juice and rind in a suitable round dish and microwave on HIGH for 4 min.
2 Stir in liquid sweetener, if used.
3 Peel the pears, but leave them whole with their stalks on.
4 Place the pears, standing upright, around the outside of the dish and coat immediately with the lemon liquid to prevent discolouration.
5 Cover the dish and microwave on HIGH for about 5–6 min or until pears are tender. Baste with the liquid after 3 min and rotate dish if the oven does not have a turntable.
6 Spike the cooked pears with the flaked almonds and serve either hot or cold.

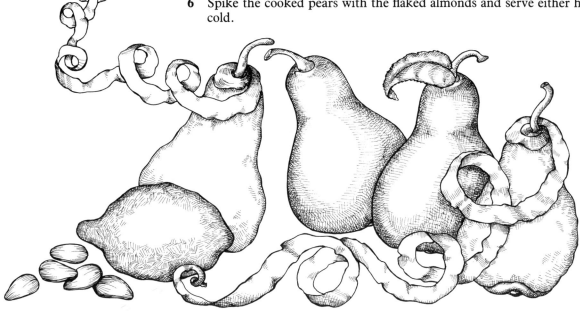

Fruit jelly mould (serves 4)

CALORIES: 216–218 (depending on options)

1 Pour the unsweetened orange juice into a measuring jug, add the drained juice from the fruit and make up to 550ml (1pt) with water.
2 Sprinkle the gelatine into the water in a suitable cup or small bowl and leave to soak for a few minutes.
3 Microwave on HIGH for 20–30 sec to dissolve. Stir, watch carefully and do not allow to boil.
4 Stir the dissolved gelatine into the fruit juice.
5 Pour a little of the liquid into the bottom of a rinsed mould and refrigerate until set.
6 Arrange a layer of fruit over the set jelly and carefully spoon some liquid jelly on top of the fruit. Refrigerate until set.
7 Add a layer of clear jelly and leave until set.
8 Continue layering fruit and jelly in this way until all the fruit has been used, finishing with a layer of clear jelly.
9 Refrigerate until firmly set.
10 Unmould and serve either alone or with orange segments and yoghurt, if liked.

VARIATION
Set the clear jelly in a ring mould. Turn out on to a serving plate and fill the centre with the fruit.

200ml (8fl oz) unsweetened natural orange juice
1 × 298g (10½oz) can mandarins in natural juice, drained
1 × 15g (½oz) sachet powdered gelatine
2 × 15ml tbsp (2tbsp) water
orange segments (optional)
natural or mandarin low-fat yoghurt (optional)

Low-fat yoghurt

CALORIES: 234

1 Fill a Thermos flask or insulated jar with hot water and leave to keep warm.
2 Place the dried skimmed milk powder in a 1 litre (1¾pt) Pyrex measuring jug and mix with 2 × 15ml tbsp (2tbsp) of the measured liquid milk until smooth.
3 Gradually stir in the rest of liquid milk.
4 Microwave gently on LOW for about 6–8 min or until the temperature of the milk reaches 60°C (140°F).
5 Stir and leave to cool to 50°C (122°F).
6 Mix a little of the cooled milk into the yoghurt and then gradually add the rest of the milk. The temperature of this mixture should now be 45°C (113°F).
7 Empty the hot water out of the flask or jar, draining thoroughly, and pour in the yoghurt mixture. Secure lid closures firmly in position.
8 Leave the sealed flask or jar in a warm place, such as an airing cupboard, for at least 8 hours to set.
9 Turn out into a bowl and beat until smooth. Refrigerate until cold.
10 The yoghurt is now ready for use. It can also be stored, covered, in the coldest part of a refrigerator where it should keep for 2–4 days and can be used in sweet and savoury recipes requiring natural yoghurt in this book.

VARIATIONS
Add fresh, stewed, or low-calorie canned fruits to the yoghurt and serve, chilled, in individual dishes.
Add artificial sweetener to taste and serve with fresh fruit salad, stewed fruit or desserts instead of cream.

1 × 15ml tbsp (1tbsp) low-fat dried skimmed milk powder
550ml (1pt) liquid skimmed milk
1 × 15ml tbsp (1tbsp) natural low-fat yoghurt, commercially prepared

Cooking for one

It is easy to convince yourself that it is not worth cooking for one. For slimmers this can spell disaster since highly fattening snacks or nibbles are neither nutritionally sound nor do they ward off hunger pangs for long. With a microwave oven there is no excuse for snack eating because high-protein, nourishing, low-calorie dishes can be prepared in minutes, whether you are at home alone at mealtimes, or cooking separate menus for yourself to be eaten at family meals.

It is a good idea, particularly when slimming, to prepare and cook food ahead of mealtimes, ready to reheat quickly in the microwave oven and eat when you are hungry. To save even more time, cook larger quantities at a time, package and freeze in individual portions, ready to defrost or reheat in the oven. This means that you can have a wide variety of portion-controlled slimmer's dishes permanently at hand and only minutes away from the dining table. With a microwave oven, therefore, there is absolutely no excuse for not eating sensibly and healthily.

With all microwave cooking, timing is directly related to the amount of food being cooked, so smaller single portions will cook very quickly and must be tested and checked carefully. Always underestimate the defrosting, reheating or cooking times. Food can always be returned to the microwave oven if necessary, but there is no remedy for overcooked food. Try some of the recipes in this section, and soon you will be substituting or adapting them to provide even more variety.

150–225g (5–8oz) smoked
   haddock
2 × 15ml tbsp (2tbsp) skimmed
   milk

Poached haddock *colour opposite*
CALORIES: 184–242 *(depending on weight)*

1 Lay fish in a shallow individual serving dish. Spoon the milk over the fish.
2 Cover and cook on HIGH for about 3–4 min, depending on the actual weight and thickness of the fish. Do not overcook.
3 Stand, covered, for 2 min. Serve, either on its own or with a poached egg on top.

1 egg
2 slices bacon, derinded

Baked egg with bacon
CALORIES: 180

1 Break egg on to a saucer, prick the yolk and cover with plastic wrap.
2 Microwave on HIGH for about 1½–2½ min, depending on personal preference. Leave to stand, covered.
3 Meanwhile, snip the bacon fat to prevent curling and place the slices between double-thickness absorbent kitchen paper on a suitable serving plate. The paper will absorb the fat during cooking.
4 Microwave on HIGH for 2–2½ min or until cooked as preferred. Turn the plate after 1 min if the oven does not have a turntable.
5 Remove the greasy kitchen paper, leaving the bacon on the plate and transfer the egg from the saucer to the plate.

VARIATION
Omit the bacon and cook only the egg—or 2 eggs.

Crispy Fish Fingers in microwave browning dish (page 106); Poached Haddock (above)

2 slices streaky bacon, derinded
1 egg
1 tomato, halved

Grilled bacon, egg and tomato

CALORIES: 188

1 Pre-heat a microwave browning dish following the manufacturer's instructions.
2 Place the bacon in the centre of the pre-heated dish and microwave on HIGH for 1–1½ min or until brown on the underside.
3 Turn the bacon over and move towards the sides of the dish.
4 Break the egg into the centre of the dish and pierce the yolk. Place the tomato halves on either side of the egg.
5 Microwave on HIGH for 1–2 min or until cooked as preferred.

2 eggs, 55–60g (grade 4)
2 × 15ml tbsp (2tbsp) water
salt and pepper
1 × 15ml tbsp (1tbsp) grated
   smoked austrian cheese
1 tomato, thinly sliced

Open cheese omelette

CALORIES: 207

1 Spray a 21.5–22.5cm (8½–9in) diameter Pyrex or suitable serving plate with low-calorie vegetable cooking spray.
2 Beat together the eggs, water and seasoning with a fork and mix well.
3 Pour the mixture on to the greased plate.
4 Microwave on HIGH for 45 sec. Using a fork, draw the set mixture around the outside of the plate to the centre, allowing the liquid egg to run to the outside.
5 Microwave on HIGH for a further 45 sec and again draw the cooked mixture to the centre.
6 Microwave on HIGH for about a further 30 sec.
7 Sprinkle surface with grated cheese, arrange the tomato slices down the centre and microwave on HIGH for about 15–30 sec to melt the cheese and heat the tomato.
8 Serve on the cooking plate.

VARIATIONS
Substitute 1 × 15ml tbsp (1tbsp) chopped ham, finely chopped chives, or crumbled cooked bacon for the cheese.

1 × 120g (4¼oz) can sardines
   in tomato sauce
1–2 slices low-calorie bread,
   toasted conventionally
lemon slices
parsley

Sardines on toast

CALORIES: 245–280 (*depending on bread slices*)

1 Remove bones from sardines and place in a small bowl with the tomato sauce. Cover.
2 Make toast and keep warm.
3 Microwave the sardines on HIGH for 30–60 sec.
4 Pile on the hot toast, pour the sauce on top, and garnish with lemon slices and chopped parsley.

1 × 150g (5oz) sirloin steak

Browning dish sirloin

CALORIES: 330

1 Slash fat edge of steak at 2.5cm (1in) intervals to prevent curling.
2 Pre-heat a microwave browning dish, following the manufacturer's instructions.
3 Place the steak in the dish and microwave on HIGH for 1½–2 min.
4 Turn steak over and microwave on HIGH for a further 1½–3½ min, or until steak is cooked rare, medium or well done, as preferred.

Commercially frozen individual 'cook-in-the-bag' fish and meat

FISH
1 Pierce a small hole in the top of the pack and place on a serving plate.
2 Microwave on LOW for 6 min. Stand for 2 min. Microwave on LOW for a further 5 min.
3 Shake bag gently before serving.

MEAT
1 Slit top of pack with scissors and place on a serving plate.
2 Microwave on HIGH for about 5 min, shaking the bag after about 2 min.
3 Leave to stand for 2 min and shake bag gently before serving.

cod in butter, cheese, parsley or shrimp sauce, 170g (6oz) pack (175–195 calories)
plaice in cream sauce, 170g (6oz) pack (175 calories)
smoked cod in butter sauce, 170g (6oz) pack (195 calories)

beef casserole with dumplings, 213g (7½oz) pack (240 calories)
braised kidneys in gravy, 142g (5oz) pack (200 calories)
gravy and lean roast beef, 113g (4oz) pack (95 calories)
gravy and roast chicken, 113g (4oz) pack (190 calories)
gravy and roast leg of pork, 113g (4oz) pack (280 calories)
chicken and vegetable casserole, 170g (6oz) pack (160 calories)
chicken and mushroom casserole (colour page 23), 170g (6oz) pack (160 calories)
liver with onion and gravy, 142g (5oz) pack (190 calories)
minced beef and vegetables in gravy, 170g (6oz) pack (150 calories)

Sautéed kidneys
CALORIES: 386

1 Toss the chopped kidneys lightly in a little seasoned flour.
2 Melt the fat in a suitable dish on HIGH for 30–45 sec.
3 Add the onion, cover and cook on HIGH for 45–60 sec.
4 Stir in the kidneys, cover and cook on HIGH for about 4 min.
5 Serve on a bed of freshly cooked cabbage or on toast.

4 lamb's kidneys, skinned, cored and finely chopped
seasoned flour
25g (1oz) low-fat spread
1 small onion, finely chopped
cooked cabbage or low-calorie bread, toasted conventionally

Scrambled eggs with chives *colour page 29*
CALORIES: 205

1 Beat the eggs and milk or water together in a 550ml (1pt) Pyrex jug. Stir in seasoning and chives.
2 Microwave on HIGH for about 1½ min, stirring every 30 sec.
3 Serve, if liked, on hot toasted bread.

VARIATIONS
Substitute finely chopped onion, chopped parsley, or sliced mushrooms for chives, or flavour with herbs.

2 eggs
2 × 15ml tbsp (2tbsp) skimmed milk, water, or milk and water mixed
salt and pepper
1 × 15ml tbsp (1tbsp) chopped chives
1 slice toasted low-calorie bread (optional)

1 × quarter chicken joint,
    weighing 200–225g (7–8oz)
1 × 35g (1¼oz) sachet seasoned
    coating mix for chicken

Crisp coated chicken
CALORIES: 165

1 Pre-heat a microwave browning dish, following the manufacturer's instructions.
2 Skin the chicken joint, remove any fat and dip in the seasoned coating mix.
3 Place joint in browning dish and microwave on HIGH for 5 min.
4 Turn joint over and microwave on HIGH for about 5–7 min or until cooked.
5 Serve immediately.

4 frozen breaded cod fish
    fingers
1 medium tomato, sliced
low-calorie seafood or tartare
    sauce

Crispy fish fingers *colour page 103*
CALORIES: 228

1 Pre-heat a microwave browning dish according to the manufacturer's instructions.
2 Spray surface of pre-heated dish with low-calorie vegetable oil spray.
3 Place the fish fingers on the base of the dish.
4 Microwave on HIGH for 1½ min.
5 Turn fish fingers over, add the sliced tomato and microwave on HIGH for a further 1½–2 min.
6 Serve immediately with a little low-calorie seafood or tartare sauce.

2 slices fresh pineapple,
    cut 1.25cm (½in) thick
100g (4oz) low-fat cottage
    cheese
toasted flaked almonds
    (optional)

Sweet and savoury snack lunch *colour opposite*
CALORIES: 160

1 Remove centre core from pineapple slices and spray one side with low-calorie vegetable oil spray.
2 Pre-heat a microwave browning dish following the manufacturer's instructions.
3 Place the pineapple, sprayed-side down, in the browning dish and microwave on HIGH for 1–1¼ min or until warmed and lightly browned.
4 Arrange the slices on a serving plate, fill the centres with cottage cheese and sprinkle with toasted almonds, if used.

VARIATION
If fresh pineapple is not available, use pineapple rings, canned in natural juice, drained.

100g (4oz) frozen spinach
1 egg
nutmeg
salt and pepper

Egg florentine
CALORIES: 116

1 Place the frozen spinach in a round individual serving dish.
2 Cover and microwave on HIGH for 4–5 min, stirring after 2–3 min. Drain and stir.
3 Make a depression in the centre of the spinach, break an egg into the well and pierce the yolk.
4 Sprinkle with nutmeg, cover with clingfilm and cook on LOW for about 2–2½ min or until egg is cooked as preferred. Do not overcook.
5 Stand, covered, for 2 min.
6 Season and serve.

*Sweet and Savoury Snack Lunch
(above)*

VARIATION
For less strict slimmers, serve topped with cheese sauce, without the nutmeg.

Entertaining

So many people nowadays are weight-conscious that most likely at least one of your guests will be on a diet. This does not mean that meals need to be dull or uninspiring. With the help of a microwave oven and the many low-calorie basic ingredients on the market today, low-calorie meals can be as attractive, appetising and enjoyable as calorie-laden menus which leave you feeling unhealthily overfull and guilty.

Plan meals carefully, choosing a low-calorie starter to allow more scope for the main course, and finish with either a light dessert or simply fresh fruit. Additional extras or accompaniments to each course can be provided for those who are not weight-conscious, and if you feel a cheeseboard is essential, do include the lower-calorie cheeses such as edam, brie, camembert and smoked austrian, all of which are delicious with fresh fruit—and preferable to the more usual high-calorie buttered biscuits.

With a microwave oven, meals for guests can be planned and cooked well in advance and reheated quickly at the last minute—yet taste freshly cooked. The speed of the microwave, together with its ability to cook such a wide variety of foods in their own juices, without fat and without the need for calorie-laden rich sauces and accompaniments, makes entertaining a pleasure and ensures compliments for the hostess. As well as the recipes in this section, you will find that many others throughout the book are suitable for entertaining.

Chicken liver pâté *(serves 6)* *colour page 111*
CALORIES: 845

450g (1lb) chicken livers
1 medium onion, skinned and finely chopped
1 × 213g (7½oz) can mushrooms in brine, drained
1 clove garlic finely chopped
salt
pinch of cayenne pepper
1 × 5ml tsp (1tsp) prepared mustard
50ml (2fl oz) chicken stock, or brandy
50g (2oz) low-fat spread (optional)

1 Mix all the ingredients together in a suitable casserole or bowl.
2 Cover and microwave on LOW for about 18–20 min or until livers are cooked.
3 Place mixture in a blender and mix until smooth.
4 Turn into a serving dish or individual dishes, cool and refrigerate.
5 Garnish with gherkin fans, juniper berries or sliced tomato before serving.

Courgettes provençale *(serves 4)*
CALORIES: 596

450g (1lb) courgettes, thinly sliced
1 × 397g (14oz) can peeled tomatoes, drained and chopped
salt and pepper
pinch of thyme
pinch of basil
garlic powder
100g (4oz) grated cheese
50g (2oz) breadcrumbs

1 Arrange a layer of courgettes in the bottom of a round flameproof casserole.
2 Spread the drained chopped tomatoes on top and sprinkle with the seasonings, herbs and half the grated cheese.
3 Layer with the remaining courgettes.
4 Cover and microwave on HIGH for 8–10 min or until vegetables are tender. Turn dish after 4 min if the oven does not have a turntable.
5 Mix the remaining cheese with the breadcrumbs and sprinkle on top.
6 Brown under a pre-heated conventional grill.

Scampi provençale (*serves 5–6*) *colour page 111*
CALORIES: 575

1 Place the garlic and onion in a suitable dish with 1tbsp of the tomato juice from the canned tomatoes.
2 Cover and cook on HIGH for 1½–2 min or until onion is transparent.
3 Add the drained chopped tomatoes, wine, seasoning and parsley.
4 Cover and cook on HIGH for 5 min.
5 Add the scampi or prawns, stir, cover and cook on HIGH for 3 min.
6 Stir well, separating the scampi or prawns if necessary.
7 Cover and continue cooking on HIGH for a further 2–3 min or until piping hot.
8 Serve with plain boiled rice.

1 clove garlic, crushed or finely chopped
1 medium onion, skinned and finely chopped
1 × 397g (14oz) can peeled tomatoes, drained and chopped
4 × 15ml tbsp (4tbsp) dry white wine
salt and pepper
1 × 15ml tbsp (1tbsp) finely chopped parsley
450g (1lb) frozen unbreaded scampi or Dublin Bay prawns

Lobster tails (*serves 2–4*)
CALORIES: 297–393 (*depending on weight*)

1 Place frozen lobster, in original wrapping, in a shallow dish.
2 Microwave on LOW for about 6–8 min to defrost partially.
3 Leave to stand for 10–15 min or until thoroughly defrosted.
4 Using scissors, cut the top shell in half lengthways.
5 Release the flesh and, leaving it connected to the shell at the tail end, pull the meat through the slit and place on top of the shell.
6 Arrange the tails in a suitable shallow dish, flesh-side uppermost and brush with the melted fat and lemon juice.
7 Cover and microwave on HIGH for about 6–7 min or until flesh is opaque and shell turns red.
8 Serve sprinkled with paprika, if used, accompanied by lemon wedges.

4 frozen lobster tails, weighing 450–675g (1–1½lb)
25g (1oz) melted low-fat spread or butter
1 × 5ml tsp (1tsp) lemon juice
paprika (optional)
lemon wedges

Note To cook 1 lobster tail, microwave on HIGH for 2½–3 min or until flesh is opaque and shell turns red.

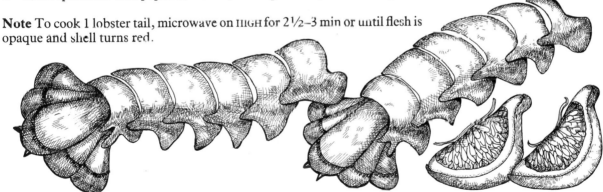

Stuffed tomatoes (*serves 6 as a starter*)
CALORIES: 380

1 Slice tops off tomatoes and reserve.
2 Carefully spoon out the tomato flesh and mix with remaining ingredients.
3 Fill the tomatoes with the mixture and replace the tops.
4 Arrange the tomatoes in a circle on a plate.
5 Microwave on HIGH for about 4–6 min, turning plate round after 2 min if the oven does not have a turntable.

6 large tomatoes
50g (2oz) chicken liver pâté
50g (2oz) lean chopped ham
3 × 15ml tbsp (3tbsp) boiled rice
2 × 5ml tsp (2tsp) horseradish sauce
salt and pepper

2 × 15ml tbsp (2tbsp) cornflour
425ml (¾pt) skimmed milk
425ml (¾pt) boiling stock
1 × 170g (6oz) can crabmeat, drained
1 × 326g (11½oz) can sweetcorn, drained
50ml (2fl oz) natural low-fat yoghurt or single cream
salt and pepper

Crab and corn soup *(serves 4–5)*
CALORIES: 648

1 Make a white sauce with the cornflour and skimmed milk on HIGH (see page 37).
2 Gradually stir in the boiling stock.
3 Break up the drained crabmeat into small pieces and add with the drained corn, salt and pepper.
4 Cover and microwave on LOW for 6–7 min, or until heated through, stirring after 3 min.
5 Fold in yoghurt or cream just before serving.

4 × 225–275g (8–10oz) trout
salt and pepper
lemon juice
25g (1oz) toasted flaked almonds
few green grapes, halved and stoned
lemon wedges

Trout with almonds and grapes *(serves 4)*
CALORIES: 960

1 Lay the trout in a dish in a single layer and either overlap the tails or shield them by wrapping in small pieces of foil to prevent overcooking.
2 Score the skin to prevent bursting and cover the dish.
3 Microwave on HIGH for about 9–12 min or until fish is cooked when tested at the thickest part.
4 Leave to stand, covered, for 2–3 min.
5 Remove foil, if used, and sprinkle trout with toasted flaked almonds.
6 Garnish with the grapes and lemon wedges.
7 Serve as a main course with a side-salad.

8–12 good-sized mushrooms, cleaned
15g (½oz) low-fat spread
25g (1oz) blue cheese, crumbled
1 × 15ml tbsp (1tbsp) browned breadcrumbs
chopped parsley

Blue cheese mushrooms *(serves 4 as a starter)*
CALORIES: 226

1 Remove stems from mushrooms and chop finely.
2 Place chopped stems and low-fat spread in a suitable dish and cook on HIGH for 1–1½ min.
3 Stir in cheese and breadcrumbs, mixing well together.
4 Spoon the mixture into the caps and sprinkle with parsley.
5 Arrange the filled caps on a plate and microwave on HIGH for 2–3 min or until hot.

2 whole plaice, filleted and skinned (ie 8 fillets)
1 × 15ml tbsp (1tbsp) cornflour
275ml (½pt) skimmed milk
salt and pepper
2 × 5ml tsp (2tsp) lemon juice
2 egg yolks, beaten
cayenne pepper
100g (4oz) green seedless grapes, skinned and halved

Plaice véronique *(serves 4)*
CALORIES: 752

1 Roll up each fillet from head to tail, skin-side inside.
2 Arrange close together in a single layer in a shallow dish.
3 Cover and microwave on HIGH for about 8–10 min, rotating the dish during the cooking period if the oven does not have a turntable.
4 Carefully drain off the cooking liquor and reserve.
5 Blend the cornflour with the milk, add the strained cooking liquor and season.
6 Cook the sauce on HIGH for 2½–3 min, stirring every minute.
7 Whisk in the lemon juice and cook on HIGH for a further minute or until thickened.
8 Whisk in egg yolks and adjust seasoning if necessary.
9 Arrange the cooked fillets on a warm serving dish and coat each one with a little sauce, serving the remainder separately.
10 Garnish with a little cayenne pepper and decorate with the skinned, halved grapes.

Scampi Provençale with Rice (page 109); Chicken Liver Pâté (page 108)

1 × 170g (6oz) packet buttered
  kipper fillets, frozen
225g (8oz) low-fat cottage
  cheese, natural or with chives
15g (½oz) powdered gelatine
150ml (¼pt) water
salt and pepper
thinly sliced cucumber, radish
  and cress to garnish

Kipper mousse (*serves 4*)
CALORIES: 589

1 Using scissors, make a small slit in the top of the fish pack.
2 Place on a plate and microwave on HIGH for 5 min.
3 Remove kippers from pack, draining off excess butter. Cool, skin and flake.
4 Sprinkle the gelatine over the water in a small bowl and leave to soak for a few minutes.
5 Microwave on HIGH for a few seconds only until gelatine is dissolved. Stir.
6 Place kipper flesh, cottage cheese and dissolved gelatine in a liquidiser and blend until smooth. Season to taste.
7 Turn the mixture into a 450g (1lb) loaf tin which has been lightly greased with low-fat spread.
8 Refrigerate the mousse until completely set and firm.
9 Turn out on to a serving dish and garnish with the cucumber, radish and cress before serving as a starter or cold buffet dish.

1 × 1kg (2lb) piece of fresh
  middle-cut salmon
8 × 15ml tbsp (8tbsp) water
1 × 15ml tbsp (1tbsp) lemon
  juice
salt and pepper
low-calorie seafood sauce

Poached salmon (*serves 5–6*)
CALORIES: 1,440

1 Place the salmon in a fairly shallow round dish about 25cm (10in) in diameter.
2 Slit the skin in 2–3 places to allow steam to escape during cooking and prevent bursting.
3 If necessary, secure flap of skin in position with wooden cocktail sticks to give fish a good shape.
4 Mix together the water, lemon juice and seasoning.
5 Pour the seasoned liquid over the fish and cover the dish with clingfilm.
6 Microwave on HIGH for 3 min, turn fish over and continue on HIGH for a further 3–5 min or until flesh is opaque and cooked in the centre. Do not overcook.
7 Leave to stand, covered, until cold. Refrigerate and serve chilled with low-calorie seafood sauce, mixed salad, and boiled new potatoes for guests.

1kg (2lb) sole fillets
1 shallot, sliced
salt and pepper
100ml (4fl oz) dry white wine
100g (4oz) small button
  mushroom caps

Sauce
50ml (2fl oz) skimmed milk
1 × 15ml tbsp (1tbsp) cornflour
salt and pepper
200ml (8fl oz) reserved
  poaching liquid
1 × 15ml tbsp (1tbsp) lemon
  juice
1 × 15ml tbsp (1tbsp) chopped
  parsley

Fillets of sole bonne femme (*serves 6–8*)
CALORIES: 897

1 Arrange the fish fillets in a suitable dish with the thicker parts towards the outside.
2 Sprinkle the onion, seasoning and wine over the fish.
3 Cover and microwave on HIGH for about 10–12 min or until fish flakes easily. Drain and reserve liquid for sauce.
4 Place the mushrooms in a bowl, cover and microwave on HIGH for about 1½–2 min or until cooked.
5 Arrange the mushrooms over the cooked fish. Stand, covered, to keep warm.
6 Blend the cornflour with the milk and add the seasoning and reserved poaching liquid, beating until smooth.
7 Microwave the sauce on HIGH for about 3 min or until thickened. Stir during cooking.
8 Beat in the lemon juice and parsley.
9 Pour the sauce over the fish and mushrooms and, if necessary, reheat for 1–2 min on HIGH before serving.

Glazed ham piquant (*serves 4*)

CALORIES: 715

1 Turn the ham into a suitable serving dish and spoon over 4 × 15ml tbsp (4tbsp) fruit juice.
2 Mix together the mustard and cinnamon and brush this mixture over the top of the ham.
3 Cover and microwave on HIGH for 6–8 min or until heated through. Add the apricots for the final minute if these are preferred warm. Rotate the dish during the heating period if the oven does not have a turntable.
4 Stud the ham with cloves and garnish with the apricots and watercress before serving.

VARIATION
Serve cold on a bed of lettuce garnished with the apricots and watercress.

1 × 454g (16oz) can of ham
1 × 198g (7oz) can apricots in natural juice, drained
2 × 5ml tsp (2tsp) french mustard
pinch of cinnamon
cloves
watercress

Cheese and cucumber ring (*serves 5–6*)

CALORIES: 358

1 Cut about 24 thin slices from the cucumber and reserve for decoration.
2 Grate the remaining cucumber fairly coarsely into a bowl and drain off liquid.
3 Stir in the yoghurt, vinegar, cottage cheese and season to taste.
4 Place the water in a suitable small bowl and sprinkle in the gelatine. Leave to soak for a few minutes.
5 Microwave on HIGH for 15–30 sec, then stir until gelatine has dissolved. Do not allow to boil.
6 Stir the dissolved gelatine into the prepared mixture and turn into a 500ml (1pt) ring mould which has been greased with low-calorie vegetable oil spray.
7 Refrigerate for a few hours until firmly set.
8 Loosen the sides of the mould with a knife and turn out on to a serving plate.
9 Decorate around the outside with overlapping slices of reserved cucumber.
10 Serve as a starter, or with mixed salad as a light lunch or supper dish.

VARIATION
Substitute 225g (8oz) cottage cheese with salmon and cucumber for the cottage cheese varieties suggested above. Fill the centre with drained canned salmon and serve with salad as a more substantial main course dish.

1 large cucumber
150ml (5fl oz) natural low-fat yoghurt
1 × 5ml tsp (1tsp) white or cider vinegar
1 × 226g (8oz) carton cottage cheese, either natural, with chives, or with peppers and onions
salt and pepper
1 × 15g (½oz) sachet powdered gelatine
2 × 15ml tbsp (2tbsp) water

Grapefruit wellington (*serves 4*)

CALORIES: 147

1 Cut grapefruit in half, loosen the segments with a serrated knife and remove pips.
2 Make a water-lily effect with scissors on the outer rim of the fruit.
3 Place in individual serving dishes, pour over the sherry and sugar, if used.
4 Arrange in a circle in the oven and microwave on HIGH for 2½–3½ min.
5 Serve decorated with half a cherry in the centre of each one.

Note
Sugar can be offered separately if it was not used in cooking.

2 grapefruit
4 × 15ml tbsp (4tbsp) dry sherry
brown sugar (optional)
2 maraschino cherries, drained and halved

175g (6oz) sliced mushrooms
1 medium onion, peeled and
  sliced
1 × 283g (10oz) can
  beansprouts, drained
100g (4oz) cooked ham,
  chopped
1 level 15ml tbsp (1 level tbsp)
  cornflour
150ml (¼pt) water
1 × 15ml tbsp (1tbsp) dry
  sherry, (optional)
1 × 15ml tbsp (1tbsp) soy sauce
salt and pepper
watercress or parsley sprigs

Ham, mushroom and beansprout entrée *(serves 4–6)*

CALORIES: 302

1   Place the mushrooms and onion in a suitable dish or casserole, cover and cook on HIGH for 3 min.
2   Stir in the drained beansprouts and ham.
3   Blend the cornflour to a smooth paste with a little of the measured water. Add the remaining water, sherry, if used, and soy sauce.
4   Stir this liquid into the vegetable and ham mixture and season to taste.
5   Cover and microwave on HIGH for about 4–5 min or until thoroughly heated. Stir during heating.
6   Stand, covered, for 2–3 min before serving from the dish or in individual dishes, garnished with watercress or parsley sprigs.

450g (1lb) onions, peeled and
  sliced
2 × 15ml tbsp (2tbsp) water
675g (1½lb) potatoes, peeled
  and cut into 0.5cm (¼in)
  thick slices
salt and pepper
chopped chives or parsley

Lyonnaise-style potatoes *(serves 6)*

CALORIES: 592 *(768 with cheese topping)*

1   Place the onions and water in a large, fairly shallow flameproof dish.
2   Cover and microwave on HIGH for 5 min, stirring during cooking.
3   Drain the onions and reserve the cooking liquid.
4   Arrange the potatoes and onions in alternate layers in the dish, ending with a layer of potato slices, and seasoning the layers.
5   Pour over the reserved cooking liquid and cover the dish with clingfilm.
6   Microwave on HIGH for about 15 min or until the potatoes are cooked. Test after 12 min and turn the dish regularly during cooking if the oven does not have a turntable.
7   Stand, covered, for a few minutes.
8   Remove cover, brown under a pre-heated conventional grill and serve sprinkled with chopped chives or parsley.

VARIATION
To serve as a family main course dish rather than as an accompanying vegetable, sprinkle the top with 50g (2oz) grated cheese before browning under the grill.

675g (1½lb) mixed soft fruits
  such as strawberries,
  raspberries, blackberries,
  blackcurrants
1 × 15ml tbsp (1tbsp) clear
  honey
6–8 slices wholemeal or low-
  calorie bread, cut 1.25cm
  (½in) thick
natural low-fat yoghurt
  (optional)

Healthy summer pudding *(serves 4–6)*

CALORIES: 396

1   Reserve a little of the mixed fruits and place the remainder with the honey in a large bowl or casserole.
2   Cover and microwave on HIGH for about 4–5 min or until the juices begin to run from the fruit. Shake or stir gently during cooking without breaking the fruit.
3   Line the base and sides of a 1 litre (1¾pt) pudding bowl or dish with enough slices of bread to cover it, reserving some to cover the top.
4   Reserve about 2tbsp of fruit juice. Spoon the fruit and the rest of the juice into the bread-lined bowl. Cover the top with bread.
5   Lay a plate or saucer that fits inside the bowl on top of the pudding and place a heavy weight on top.
6   Refrigerate the pudding, for at least 6 hours, or preferably overnight.
7   Turn out on to a serving plate or dish, spoon over the reserved fruit juice and decorate with the reserved fruit and yoghurt, if used.

Citrus Cheesecake (page 117)

4 ripe, even-sized pears
275ml (½pt) dry red wine
50ml (2fl oz) water
few drops of lemon juice
good pinch of cinnamon or
    nutmeg
calorie-free sweetener to taste
    (optional)

Pears in red wine *(serves 4)*
CALORIES: 350

1   Peel the pears but leave them whole with their stalks on.
2   Place the wine, water, lemon juice and cinnamon or nutmeg in a suitable serving dish.
3   Cover and microwave on HIGH for about 4–5 min.
4   Add sweetener to taste, if used.
5   Arrange the pears in a single layer in the hot wine, basting them well with the liquid.
6   Cover and microwave on HIGH for 4–5 min or until just tender, but still holding their shape. Rotate the dish during cooking if the oven does not have a turntable.
7   Leave to stand for a few minutes before serving. This dish may be served cold, if preferred.

225g (8oz) blackcurrants
2 × 15ml tbsp (2tbsp) water
artificial sweetener to taste
275ml (½pt) natural
    unsweetened low-fat yoghurt
2 egg whites

Blackcurrant yoghurt sorbet *(serves 4–6)*
CALORIES: 216

1   Place the blackcurrants and water in a suitable bowl.
2   Cover and microwave on HIGH for 2 min. Shake or stir and cook for about a further minute or until soft and pulpy.
3   Cool slightly before placing in a blender and liquidising until smooth. Sieve to remove pips.
4   Add artificial sweetener to taste and leave until cold.
5   Stir in the yoghurt and fold in the stiffly beaten egg whites.
6   Turn into a suitable container and freeze.
7   Remove from the freezer about 15 min before required.
8   Scoop into tall glasses to serve.

VARIATION
Substitute other soft fruits, such as raspberries, strawberries or blackberries, and proceed as above.

116

Strawberry yoghurt whip (*serves 4–6*) *colour page 92*
CALORIES: 460

1 Place the jelly cubes with 275ml (½pt) water in a suitable measuring jug.
2 Heat on HIGH for 2–3 min or until jelly dissolves. Stir after each minute.
3 Make up to 425ml (¾pt) with cold water and leave to cool.
4 Stir the yoghurt into the cooled jelly and leave until on the point of setting.
5 Whisk until light and fluffy and turn into a large serving dish or individual dishes.
6 Chill in refrigerator until set.
7 Serve with natural yoghurt and/or fresh strawberries.

VARIATION
Substitute raspberry or blackcurrant jelly and use yoghurt the same flavour as the jelly.

1 strawberry jelly, cut into cubes
1 × 142g (5oz) carton low-fat strawberry yoghurt

Blackberry and brandy mousse (*serves 6*) *colour page 92*
CALORIES: 266

1 Reserve a few blackberries for decoration.
2 Place the remaining blackberries and the 2 × 15ml tbsp (2tbsp) water in a suitable dish.
3 Cover and microwave on HIGH for 4–5 min or until the fruit is cooked.
4 Add sweetener to taste.
5 Sprinkle the gelatine into the 4 × 15ml tbsp (4tbsp) water and leave to soak for a few minutes before stirring into the hot fruit.
6 Stir in the orange juice, yoghurt and brandy and blend together in a liquidiser.
7 Turn into a serving dish or individual dishes and chill in the refrigerator until set.
8 Decorate with reserved fruit before serving.

VARIATION
Substitute other soft fruits, such as loganberries, strawberries, raspberries or blackcurrants, and proceed as above.

450g (1lb) fresh or frozen blackberries, defrosted if frozen
2 × 15ml tbsp (2tbsp) water
calorie-free sweetener to taste
1 × 15g (½oz) sachet powdered gelatine
4 × 15ml tbsp (4tbsp) water
1 × 15ml tbsp (1tbsp) natural unsweetened orange juice
1 × 142g (5oz) carton natural low-fat yoghurt
2 × 15ml tbsp (2tbsp) brandy

Citrus cheesecake (*serves 8–10*) *colour page 115*
CALORIES: 999

1 Mix the crushed biscuits with the melted low-fat spread.
2 Spoon into a 20cm (8in) round flan dish, or lightly oiled flan ring placed on a flat plate, and spread over the base.
3 Liquidise or sieve the cottage cheese and mix with the beaten egg yolks, lemon rind and juice and yoghurt.
4 Sprinkle the gelatine into the water in a suitable small bowl.
5 Microwave on HIGH for 20–30 sec to dissolve the gelatine. Do not allow to boil. Stir well.
6 Whisk the egg whites until stiff.
7 Stir the dissolved gelatine into the cheese mixture and fold in the egg whites.
8 Turn the mixture on to the crumb base and leave to set in the refrigerator for at least 2 hours.
9 Serve straight from the flan dish, or on a plate with flan ring removed, decorated with orange segments.

Base
6 low-calorie digestive biscuits, crushed
25g (1oz) low fat spread, melted
Filling
1 × 225g (8oz) tub low-fat cottage cheese
3 eggs, separated
grated rind and juice of 1 lemon
1 × 142g (5oz) carton mandarin orange low-fat yoghurt
1 × 15g (½oz) sachet powdered gelatine
2 × 15ml tbsp (2tbsp) water
orange segments to decorate

117

Index